The 25,000 Mile Love Story

The 25,000 Mile Love Story

*The Epic Story of the Couple
Who Sacrificed Everything to
Run the World*

Serge Roetheli

For sales and licensing inquiries, please contact the publisher:

Dunham Books
63 Music Square East
Nashville, Tennessee 37203

First Edition, September 2012

Hardcover ISBN: 978-0-9851359-8-0
E-book ISBN: 978-0-9855328-0-2

Printed in the United States of America

Table of Contents

"Meaning is not something you stumble across, like the answer to a riddle or the prize in a treasure hunt. Meaning is something you build into your life. You build it out of your own past, out of your affections and loyalties, out of the experience of humankind as it is passed on to you, out of your own talent and understanding, out of the things you believe in, out of the things and people you love, out of the values for which you are willing to sacrifice something. The ingredients are there. You are the only one who can put them together into that unique pattern that will be your life. Let it be a life that has dignity and meaning for you. If it does, then the particular balance of success or failure is of less account."

—John Gardner

"When I was very young and the urge to be somewhere was upon me, I was assured by mature people that maturity would cure this itch. When years described me as mature, the remedy prescribed was middle age. In middle age I was assured that greater age would calm my fever and now that I am fifty-eight, perhaps senility will do the job. Nothing has worked. Four hoarse blasts of a ship's whistle still raise the hair on my neck and set my feet to tapping. The sound of a jet, an engine warming up, even the clopping of shod hooves on pavement brings on the ancient shudder, the dry mouth and vacant eye, the hot palms and the churn of stomach high up under the rib cage. In other words, I don't improve; in further words, once a bum always a bum. I fear the disease is incurable."

—John Steinbeck, *Travels with Charley*

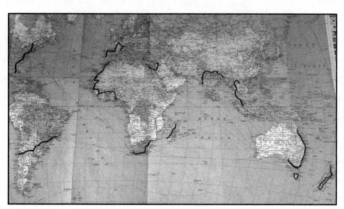

Map of the World Tour

The 25,000 Mile Love Story

Map of the American Challenge

Preface

These few lines are indeed more than just the preface of a book. They are an outpouring of love for a man and a woman, who have always managed to find the means of attaining their wildest dreams—to go farther than anyone had ever dared to go, to run longer than anyone had ever dared to run, and to do it out of passion, for themselves and for others, to live life intensely, but also out of a desire to help the most impoverished to survive.

Traversing Europe, then traversing North and South America, then circling the world. Smitten at the same time by egoism and altruism, absolutely disproportionate, like everything that they undertake.

There are those who will howl with indignation and others who will howl with admiration. Distinctly disproportionate, they can only arouse disproportionate reactions—like their risks, like their hopes, even like their naiveté, but above all, like their successes. They make uncomfortable only those who are afraid to take risks, those who are afraid to go beyond their comfort zones, and those who reassure themselves by watching the failures of others from a distance. However, Serge and Nicole did not fail... they succeeded—even masterfully—thus sending the faint-hearted back to their mediocrity. They ran around the world, journeying through life as we all should—with spirit, with our eyes and our hearts wide open.

Thanks, my friends, for showing us the way, but will we one day be capable of following you?

—**Bertrand Piccard**[1]

[1]Editor's Note: Bertrand Piccard has been a great inspiration for Serge Roetheli, and Serge considered it a profound honor that his friend, Bertrand, was at the starting point and at the finish line for his World Tour. In 1992, Bertrand Piccard won the first transatlantic balloon race. Then in 1999, he and Brian Jones made the first non-stop flight around the world in a balloon. Since 2004, he has been working on a project called Solar Impulse. Solar Impulse has already demonstrated that a solar-powered airplane can fly day and night using no fuel. His next challenge is to fly around the world in a solar-powered airplane. Chapter ten has more information on the Piccard family.

Introduction

"Nothing in this world can take the place of persistence. Talent will not; nothing is more common than unsuccessful people with talent. Genius will not; unrewarded genius is almost a proverb. Education will not; the world is full of educated derelicts. Persistence and determination alone are omnipotent. The slogan 'press on' has solved and always will solve the problems of the human race."

—Calvin Coolidge

The human body was not created to survive such adverse conditions. This is what they always say. At the beginning, before it even starts. In the middle, when there's still room to fail. Everyone anticipates the undoing because, before something happens for the first time, it's always called impossible.

It started, as all good things do, with a bet. An innkeeper in a cozy Welsh hamlet found himself bickering with a foxhunter. The question at hand? Speed. Who could run faster, man or horse? The foxhunter favored the horse. The innkeeper favored the human. Over a course of many miles, the innkeeper argued, the human would succeed. It was all about endurance.

And so, in 1981, to put matters to rest, the Man Versus Horse Marathon galloped into fruition. The race, shorter than a real marathon at just twenty-two miles, covers rough terrain and requires its competitors to be surefooted and steady. They scramble through forests, stampeding rivers, and carefully carved trails to reach the finish. In the first year, much to the innkeeper's chagrin, the four-footed competitor won in a landslide. And so it continued, year after year after year. But then, in June 2004—for the first time ever—the race took a turn; the human won.

Admittedly, not many people took notice. The Man Versus Horse Marathon doesn't clock quite as many views as the Super Bowl. But someone did see what was happening, and that someone was Dennis Bramble.

Bramble, a University of Utah biologist, along with a Harvard University paleoanthropologist named Daniel Lieberman, was in the midst of studying an important facet of human locomotion. Before the drunken Welsh argument even surfaced, the two unlikely idealists had taken the side of the innkeeper. They believed there was something remarkable about the human body and its propensity for running – particularly running long distances.

"We're loaded top to bottom with all these features, many of which don't have any role in walking," Lieberman said. In other words, they have to be intended for something. And just as much as the lion, or the antelope, or any other animal you'll find sprinting fiercely across the Sahara, there's an instinctive desire and ability in humankind to run hard, fast, and long.

Bramble and Lieberman went on to do a number of experiments, some of which are far too scientific to comprehend. One of them involved a rectal thermometer finding its way into a cheetah on a treadmill. But the overall outcome was pretty significant and likely had that Welsh innkeeper jumping in his knickers: *humans are born with the natural, God-given ability to outrun any animal on this great earth.*

I find this fascinating not only because it's just plain fascinating, but also because I love to run. I love to push my body to ends that seem uncommon and unlikely. In other words, I believe in the impossible.

I'm a mountain guide by trade. Although I was born in Zurich, in 1967 my parents moved to the town of Sion in Valais, one of the twen-

The 25,000 Mile Love Story

ty-six cantons of Switzerland, and I grew up surrounded by the glacial Rhone Valley and the pristine peak of the Matterhorn, its sides reflecting the four compass points. Valais rests in the southwest of Switzerland. To the south of it, Italy. To the southwest, France. To the sky, the Alps. Day by day, I puzzle people through the complex beauty of the Swiss terrain, the wealth of glaciers, the 4,000-meter peaks. In a world that is overly mapped and articulated, in Valais you'll find untold wildlife, isolated villages, and long-forgotten paths, where you can still get lost.

In 1986, I was in a skiing accident—not my first, as I had already had surgery on my left knee in 1982 and my right ankle in 1984—and was rushed to the hospital. The doctor inserted screws in my right knee and told me the damage was so severe that it was highly likely I would never walk again. He was sincere in his diagnosis. Steadfast. I listened to him, of course, as any good patient would. And then I promptly forgot what he said. In other words, I decided I could outrun the horse.

And that is where this story begins. At least, in many ways. With someone expecting less and life allowing more. The thing is, you can take what life gives you and be satisfied. Or you can decide that just being satisfied isn't really a very satisfactory condition.

Not only did I walk again, I ran. I ran Death Valley (100 miles); the Grand Canyon with 5,250 feet (roughly a mile) of altitude change from the rim down to the Colorado River and then back in one day; Europe in the winter, from Gibraltar to Norway (4,375 miles); Palermo, Italy to Milan (1,100 miles); and the Pan American Highway from the southern tip of Argentina to Fairbanks, Alaska in what my wife Nicole and I fondly called the American Challenge—a journey of three years and 15,000 miles. And with that, I was just getting started.

For as long as I can remember, there has always been one question that has resounded loudly in my mind, beating back doubts and carving the road for miraculous things to happen. A question that is real for every single human being, but that is far too rarely asked. What would you do if you were completely free? If you pressed yourself, how far could your legs—and, more importantly, your mind—take you? What would you see? Where would you go? Would there be enough world to cover all your aspirations?

Put simply: what were you created to accomplish?

Even now, even after everything I've experienced, the question fills my mind with wonder. When you don't confine yourself unnecessarily to the sensible, an entirely new and remarkably limitless world unfolds—a world that is tolerant of dreams.

It was two years after the American Challenge that Nicole and I decided that we would again leave our home in the Swiss village of Granois, just above the town of Sion, sell our house and all our belongings, leave behind my two precious children, Clara and Steve, along with the comfort and security of home and friends, and do the unthinkable—we would run the world. We would embark on an adventure to see—and help others see—the vastness of the world and the beauty of its inhabitants. Our goal was not just one of adventure and freedom, but also of seeing and exposing the tender aspects of the earth. In particular, children in need. By traversing the world, we could tell the story of the people we met and how they could best be helped. I would run the distance and Nicole would accompany me, riding at my side on a Yamaha motorcycle, hitched to a small trailer fitted with our necessary supplies. We would cover 25,422 miles, crossing six continents over the course of 1,910 days. And we would never, under any circumstances, give up.

It's a big idea, I know. Even now, even though it's been completed, I admit the concept sounds irrational. Too much to accomplish. To run the world!? The thought of it. But big ideas don't always start as such. They are kernels that grow and change and evolve. They start somewhere small, in a cranny of your heart, and they stretch their limbs all the way to your mind, growing from the size of mere specks and evolving into something remarkably real and tangible.

When you want to do something big, you can't be daunted by the size of the obstacle; you can't try to consume the whole feat in one bite. You have to look at it step by step, setting small, reachable goals. Throughout the World Tour, I did not think about the entire route that lay before me. That would have been brutal to my spirit. All I thought about was the thirty miles I had to run that day. If I could run thirty miles that morning and find the ability to recover my body and mind that night, then the next day I could run thirty miles again. Eventually, thirty miles a day adds up. Eventually you really can run the world.

If you're like most people, you're probably wondering what could possibly motivate anyone to run so far. What selfish conceit and ambition could fuel such a seemingly crazy act? There is a certain allure, of course, in glory. The self-satisfaction that comes with accomplishing a great feat. So many adventurers now set out because they want to be the first to accomplish something; they want to write their names on the walls of history and store up stories and photos and videos to write a book and sell a movie. The pureness of adventure escapes them.

But for me and for Nicole, our first adventures were without a camera. There was something much bigger that made the journey worthwhile and whole: our freedom to act.

Paulo Coelho once wrote, "When we least expect it, life sets us a challenge to test our courage and willingness to change; at such a moment, there is no point in pretending that nothing has happened or in saying that we are not yet ready. The challenge will not wait. Life does not look back."

I believe there is a challenge that lays before us on a daily basis. How can we be better than we were the day before? How can we stretch our boundaries and make each day meaningful—not only for ourselves, but for the people with whom we cross paths. In choosing to run the world, Nicole and I knew we were not only pressing our limits, but we would be redefining our boundaries. We would brush up against cultures and people entirely foreign to our understanding. Some would be more fortunate than us, but many others—too many others—would personally know poverty, illness, and a harsh hand of life.

Over the course of 25,000 miles, feet pounding on pavement and on jungle paths, these real-life experiences forced us to question ourselves. They stirred our hearts. They led us to modify our vision of others, to broaden our minds, and, inevitably, they forced us to change our habits.

To run the world sounds magical, an adventure of truly epic proportions. And as you will read in the pages to come, it was. But by deciding one day to change the course of our lives, to leave and run the world as we did, we also chose to give many things up. There is a price to pay for your dreams, and it is not always a small one.

For five years, we made the decision to leave behind our families, our friends, our certainties, and our comfort. We couldn't cook dinner in our kitchen or have coffee in our town square. We couldn't go to the supermarket or spend a weekend away with the kids. And over the course of those years, Nicole and I had numerous reasons to want to quit the journey—illness, car accidents, injuries, weather, and countries caught in the landslide of war. The list goes on and on. But as we learned many times along the rough road of life, the most rewarding experiences are not meant to be easy. There will be trials—both physical and emotional. There will be times when you want to quit or when those who surround you will make you question your resolve. But you must take to the road again. You must tighten your laces, strengthen your resolve, and see the course through.

There is no miracle formula; no set of ten magical steps. But there is the human choice to accept a challenge. When you decide to act, that in itself is a victory. Each day that you show up and are willing to confront your fears and persevere, you have already won.

Nicole used to say that adventure is all around; you only need look for it. And she is right. This is a book about our love of adventure, love of freedom, love of nature, love of kids, and love of each other. It's about how it happened, why it happened, and why I hope it will never stop happening. Not just to me, but also to you.

In these pages, I will take you on the road with me. While the World Tour might have been five years and 25,000 miles, in truth it has been much longer than that. It has been my whole life. It has been every step from my infancy until now, with maturity and the faint streaks of gray showing through. This is a love story, but not in the traditional sense. It is not just about a man and woman, a husband and wife. There are plenty of people who can write that story better than I. Instead, this is about a love that has lasted a lifetime—a love for the world's roads and all the people who inhabit them. You will follow me through my childhood backyard as I scrambled through the forests. You will be with me as I took up boxing and grew up into a mountain guide. You will sit by my side as I fell in love—not once, not twice, but three times. And you will run the road with me on the American Challenge and the World Tour. Then, at the end of the day, you will return with me to where I belong, and I pray that you will take away some life lessons and the truth I have come to know so well.

It doesn't matter where you come from or what you start with. Possessing more or less doesn't ensure happiness or even victory.

You cannot win the race overnight. You win it by persistence—by daily devotion. You win it by doing the little things well. *You win the race by believing you can outrun the horse.*

PART ONE

The Roots

CHAPTER ONE

He Will Live or He Will Die

"Human beings are not born once and for all on the day their mothers give birth to them, but... life obliges them over and over again to give birth to themselves."

—Gabriel Garcia Marquez

I was born on the sidewalk between a taxicab and the hospital door. A strange beginning to be sure. An indicator perhaps of what the rest of my life would be like—a rush to get going and see all there is to see. I've never been much for... what's the word? Patience. Yes, patience.

It was May 8, 1955. It started very strangely. My parents and older brother, who was only three at the time, had gone to Zurich on holiday. They were planning to go to the circus, or cirque as we say, for the night, but my mother was six and a half months pregnant and was very tired—probably from having to carry such an energetic baby around in her tummy!—and she decided to stay in. She ushered my father and brother out the door with her strict, stubborn tone (a tone I will always remember), and remained behind to rest.

Only there wouldn't be much resting. Not long after my father and brother left for a night of fanciful brightness and delightful trickery, her water broke. Most women I know would have been entirely scared out of their minds. They would have been sending bellhops and helicopters and strangers to fetch their husbands, pulling them by their ties to their hospital beds. But not my mother. She was never one to make a fuss. Always composed, always powerful, she simply went down to the lobby, got in a taxicab as though she were going out for a bag of apples, and directed the driver to the hospital. "I'm having a child," she said. "If you could be quick about it, that would be best."

The driver, truth be told, was a bit mad. He was far more caught up in the urgency of the moment than my mother. He was speeding, careening, pulling his hair out by the very fringes of his fingertips, while my mother sat in the back inhaling and exhaling.

"He's coming," she said calmly, and indeed I was.

Despite how quickly the taxicab driver sped across the freshly rained-upon streets, the speed was not enough. Half way out of the taxi, directly in front of the hospital, I came sliding out, a tiny smidgeon of a child who was born on the world's streets. A fitting delivery upon reflection of who I would become, or was it why I became who I am and what I have been.

I was small, of course, being a full two and a half months premature. Too light, in fact. One kilo and 310 grams to be exact. That's 2.88 pounds. But despite my diminutive nature, I was there, crying and yawning and stretching my limbs like any newborn baby.

I was a great surprise to my father and brother when they came home from the cirque. They had left with my mother six and a half months pregnant and had come back to a new family member.

"Heavens!" my father said, throwing up his hands. "Could he not wait!" and then he bent over and gave me a kiss. And as simply as that, I was christened as the child who causes a ruckus—a title I maintain even now as a fifty-seven year old man!

At two and a half months early, it was no surprise my family wasn't ready for me. But ready or not, there I was. They had to do something. And so they welcomed me with what they had: love.

My impossibly small size was a worry to the doctors from day one, and I stayed in a wing of the hospital for premature babies for a solid fourteen months after my birth. I was struggling to stay alive, daily fighting to get to the next day, and inevitably my mother and father had to make the call. The doctors stood by my parents in their pressed white uniforms, putting their fingers to their lips, worried. *He should stay*, they said. *To leave is to risk his life.* But my parents knew two things. One, long-term hospitalization was no real form of life at all, and two, at some point the bills would become impossible to afford. They had to take my life in their hands and make a choice.

"Serge is coming with us," my mother said, decisively as ever, and she signed a paper attesting to the fact that they took full responsibility for this decision and my health. Then she slung me, her too-small child, under her arm and walked out the door saying, "He will live or he will die; it is a risk we have to take." And that moment alone tells you a great deal about the spirit of my parents and the philosophy I was raised with. Rewards do not come without risks. Full, healthy lives do not come by sitting idly by. Sometimes in life the only option is to adapt, and the only choice is the attitude you will bring with it. And this attitude was a big thing starting from the beginning. The decision to make do, to keep going, to survive.

My brother has always said my powerful spirit to survive under any condition started that very day I was born and continued when my mother took me out of the hospital. And maybe that makes sense. For most people, life has its swells of excitement, but for the most part, for the day-to-day, they linger in normalcy. It is not a bad way of life; it is just a steady way. But for me, for my spirit that came sliding out onto the sidewalk, life is always a challenge. Sometimes glorious. Sometimes difficult. Always risky. But no matter the occasion, I always try to be a winner. And I think my mother knew that about me, too, when she walked out that hospital door.

CHAPTER TWO

Inheritance

*"If growing up means it would be beneath my dignity to climb a tree,
I'll never grow up, never grow up, never grow up! Not me!"*

—J.M. Barrie

If there's someone you want to blame for my obstinacy, it's certainly my mother. She was such a strong woman. Too strong, probably. A force likely to knock the wind straight out of you. Not once, not twice, but perpetually.

It wasn't a lack of kindness, mind you. Or a lack of caring. *She was a good mother.* It was just an absence of sugar coating that made everything very, well, real.

When my brother Yves was young, I imagine just going on ten years old, he decided he wanted to feed one of our dogs some dried apricots. My father loved dogs, so we always had one or two lurking around to play with. My mom—forever the wise one—told my brother not to give the apricots to the dog.

"He won't like them," she said assuredly.

But my brother, an inquisitive boy, said, "Of course he will. I'll just try."

Most mothers, perhaps, would have left it at that. Boys will be boys with their curiosity. But not my mother.

"Fine. Have it your way," she said. "But if you give the dog the apricots and he doesn't like them, you'll have to eat them yourself. I won't have wasted food."

My brother (foolishly) agreed to the terms and proceeded to let the pup slobber over the apricots, holding them in his mouth just for a few moments, only to spit them back out again into the dirt, disgusted by the taste. It was decidedly not Kibbles and Bits. My brother looked up helplessly at my mom, but he knew he had no choice. He picked up the slobber-coated apricots and downed them himself.

It was amusing to me, of course, in that moment. But her terseness didn't fall only on my brother. She was plenty balanced in her lesson giving.

When I was fourteen years old, I went out to build a fort in the forest. In Sion, Switzerland, where we grew up, countless trees and mountains surrounded our home. It was a natural playground for a boy's wonder and daring, and I would often go adventuring out into the abyss of nature, searching for something to excite and please me. Oftentimes, I'd end up rummaging around the trees and building a fort, pretending like I was a great conqueror of the world. In the midst of building my fort this particular time though, I decided to take a break and found a new diversion: vines. I leapt upon them with glee, swinging like Tarzan, yelping away to my heart's content. Unfortunately, the vine wasn't having as much fun as I was. I heard a ripping sound overhead and knew straight away that the end of this wouldn't be very pretty. The vine snapped, flinging me through the air and into my closest neighbor: a massive tree trunk.

I cut my arm rather severely. It was sliced wide open, and I was gushing blood. It even made me, a boy with a rather sturdy stomach, a little nauseous. I put leaves over it as best I could and started the hour-long hike back to the house.

Even though it was over forty years ago, I remember the fear very clearly. Not of the injury itself, mind you. I knew that would heal up fine. Instead I was worried about what my mother would say.

I walked in the door, leaves and blood everywhere. I was in pain and looking rather pitiful. But she wasn't alarmed. She didn't rush over to me, begging for details or asking if I was okay. Rather she took one look at me and said, "Go wash yourself up and disinfect that wound." She said it with such calmness you wouldn't imagine her son was standing straight in front of her, battered and bruised. I hated to imagine her response if she had found me coming home from war!

I did as she said, and she peered over my shoulder all the while, making sure I took care to diligently wash and sterilize the cut. She was a mother, after all, and she cared about my wellbeing, but she also wanted to make sure I understood the principles behind the lesson: there are repercussions for your decisions, so you must always be responsible for your actions. If you want to play like Tarzan in the woods, fine. Have at it. But know what can happen and be sure the action is worth the risk.

I admit I probably didn't always understand her harshness when I was growing up. And in some ways, maybe I wanted her to be a little softer. "There, Serge, there. Everything is going to be okay," would have been a welcome change. But in the end, I have to say, "Thank you, mom," because now when I decide to do something, I follow through with it. I do not falter. When I say yes, I mean yes. And when I say no, I mean no. And that's not such an easy thing really—making a promise and keeping it, particularly when you know the risks or repercussions. But my mom taught me how to be an honest man. Really, she showed me there wasn't any other way. And that is its own kind of grace, being shown so early in life the power of principle.

And more than that, of course, she gave me the ultimate lesson I've carried through life and which has proved invaluable over the course of my many adventures: you pay the price for your choices. In the end, I think maybe that distinction is what causes the chasm between the people who have many dreams and the people who are actually *doing* their dreams. When it comes down to it, many people are not willing or able to pay a huge price for their choices. They're willing only to pay a small one and so they risk little. But I'm able to pay the maximum price, because my mother was kind enough to show me a world where it was worth it. To risk it all means you can gain it all.

There is a key element here that is also crucial: Never, ever give up what you want most for what you want now. Too many people have shortsighted sensibilities. They see the immediate pain and the immediate sacrifice. What they forget is the ultimate value and prize. And when you look at situations from this nearsighted perspective, you're sure to miss out on the most valuable things in life.

I remember distinctly when I was growing up that school was a tremendous bother. I was no different than a million other kids; I dreaded going. It felt so tedious. Every day I'd ask my mom and dad, "Is it a school day or is it an off day?" The answer was rarely what I hoped.

It's not that I hated to learn, mind you. Probably quite the contrary. I loved to learn. I have an open mind and open eyes for a thousand things. But it's fair to say I didn't swallow education the way many do. I wanted to be active in it. I wanted to learn by experiment, by going outside and being in the world. Staying quiet on a chair for many hours while staring out a window was so unnatural. Then, like now, I was a nature guy. Inside a building, I feel comfortable just to spend enough time to take a shower and to get a good night's sleep, but for the rest, let me outside. My home is the sky, the mountains, the world's streets. Inside is base camp and nothing else. Inside, after two hours, I will find a reason to escape. And that was the problem in school, too. Doing the same thing as twenty other kids, over and over and over again, or just listening for hours upon hours. My God—how boring!

One day I told my mom that I wanted to stop going to school. I was in my early teens and was very adamant. I was tired of it, felt like it was a waste of time. And my mom looked at me very closely and said, "I accept your decision, Serge, but you will pay for it the rest of your life. You decide." And then she turned from me and kept slicing the onions in the kitchen.

What she said startled me and, after some thought, I realized that maybe, yes, I should keep going to school for a little while longer to learn some more. And I did. And I will always be grateful for that because while school at the time felt like an immense sacrifice, I've come to understand that education is the platform for possibility. When you have your mind sharpened and broadened, your capacity in life grows with it.

On the World Tour, I came across thousands and thousands of children who couldn't go to school. Maybe their homes were too far from the schoolhouse or maybe they couldn't afford it. Whatever it was, their hands were tied and immediately, just like that, their options in life were limited. I encouraged them as best I could, but it was when I came across the students already in the schoolhouses that I was very adamant. Persist, I said. Stick with it. If you do this, you can do anything. The lesson for them was the same as the lesson my mother taught me: never, ever give up what you want most for what you want now. Perhaps I would have had fun running in those fields rather than sitting cloistered in a room with my books. But how many fields have I now had the chance to run through due to my education? Knowing that answer always makes me smile and grateful that my mother was so tough and decisive.

My father, on the other hand, is another story. I think life was a bit too strong for him in the end. And what I remember from him, I remember from early childhood when he was at his best, before the alcohol sullied him. (Perhaps that's why I have never once indulged in alcohol.) And while he perhaps didn't leave as much of an impression on me as my mom, I don't want to miss speaking about him because he was influential in his own way. And it's because of my parents' differences, their black and white sides of the coin, that I am the way I am.

My dad died too young. Fifty-nine years old. In contrast to my mom, he brought me the sensitive, small things, the touches she couldn't possess. She had no time for little or emotional things. It's as though being affected by anything was too draining for her. But my dad was very present wherever he was. And the fact that I can now be very happy to see an alpine flower or a blue sky, or a pretty lake, or an old friend, that's evidence of my dad's character.

When I was on the World Tour, I thought a thousand times about him. It wasn't that I missed my dad exactly, but rather that I suddenly had this awareness of the gift he'd given me. It would be two o'clock in the afternoon, and Nicole and I would be setting up our tent on the side of the road. There would be nothing to do, nothing to see. Actually, nothing very extraordinary. But we'd have to stop there, because I'd already run twenty, thirty, or forty miles that day, and at a point, you have to stop somewhere. You have to let your spirit recover. Your body alone needs the rest so you can begin again tomorrow. And so you eat, you drink, you sleep, and that's it. Just a bunch of refueling. And while you might be healing your body back up, you have to learn to do the same thing with your mind. It's just as important to keep your psyche fit so you can remain powerful and accept the fact that you're hitting the road again the next morning. That's not always an easy thing.

And those were the times—in the middle of the desert, in the bareness of a cave—with nothing to occupy us, that I was immensely grateful that my father had taught me to recover my spirit and to learn to be happy with nothing.

After I turned eighteen years old, I went my own way—a path of diligence and exuberance. I became a true adventurer. But both my mom and my dad remained a distinct part of me. While perhaps I didn't see them often—particularly my father—the core truths they gave me and the love they passed on have stayed with me even to this day, long after they both have grown tired of this earth and passed away.

CHAPTER THREE

Teach Me to be a Winner

"The final forming of a person's character lies in their own hands."
—Anne Frank

People always ask me when I started running and I tell them, quite simply, it's when I started boxing. Most of them look at me funny, cocking their heads to the side like a cocker spaniel. It's not the expected answer. I guess for some reason they all think I was running marathons by age three, knocking out laps on the pavement. Only with such extremity can you run so far for so long. But that wasn't the case. I became a runner because I was a boxer, and I became a boxer because of my brother.

My older brother, Yves, was always looking out for me. He grew up too fast, probably, filling in the spaces where my dad left off. He took on that kind of parental figure, and, whether he really wanted to or not, became a guide to me. He was a pretty physically tough kid, too. The difference between us was more than just three years of age, because I was under the limit when I was born and my brother, well, he was almost over the limit, so you can imagine the chasm in size difference. When he walked into the room, there was a certain presence. Both his temperament and his size demanded you listen. I was tiny compared to him.

For me, in the first years of my life, up until I left the house, Yves and I had a very strong bond. He took me under his wing and was prodding me, constantly, to go, look, do, see. He introduced me to sports. He brought me to the mountains. He showered me with as many of life's opportunities as he could. And I wasn't the only one who could see his kindness. Everyone adored my brother. He always finished first in everything he tried to do. And he was a perfect student. I was the perfect opposite.

When we grew up and went out on our own paths, he pursued a life of adventure, just as I did. He traveled a lot, ran a lot, boxed a lot. Inevitably, he became a mountain guide, too, but it was at a different level. I was always a bit on the extreme, running out and pressing the limits. He was always more grounded, equipped with a sense of responsibility.

His sense of responsibility led me to boxing. I started training when I was fifteen years old. My brother had been going to the boxing gym for a while. My dad loved boxing and got him hooked on it, and Yves thought it would be good for me. I suppose he knew I needed some direction in my life—an outlet where I could throw all my energy into something and let it be productive. I was the kind of kid who could have started going down the wrong path and gotten lost there, but fortunately for me, Yves didn't let that happen.

I didn't want to go to the boxing gym at first. It took some convincing. I told my brother it wasn't for me. I was still too thin, perhaps a residual effect of my premature birth. And, frankly, I couldn't understand why you would want to knock in your friend's nose or face. I didn't feel comfortable with that. It seemed unkind. And so my brother said, "Okay, you don't have to be a boxer. Just come to meet some of the guys. It's a good atmosphere. We'll help you, and I'm sure you'll enjoy it." So I took his word for it, as I did most of the time, went to the gym, and discovered what ended up being a very natural calling for me.

That first year, I met my trainer, André Espinosa. He was definitely an important person in my life and stuck by my side over the course of the next twelve years. More than anyone, he brought me the capacity to receive some knocks and never give up. I trained one to two times a week those first twelve months. It was nothing intense. A boxer's training regimen often depends on where they are in their career and, since my career was non-existent, it was relatively relaxed. With beginners, like me, you start with the basics. You learn how to hit the three key bags: the heavy bag, the speed bag, and the double end bag. You build up your endurance, skipping rope, doing calisthenics, and jogging. And you do some of that shadow boxing business Muhammad Ali made famous on ABC's *Wide World of Sports*. Surprisingly, you don't do much actual boxing, though maybe a little sparring here and there. The important thing at the start is not to rush into a fight, but to condition yourself and build up the fundamentals. So that's what I did. And just as my brother said, it was a good, healthy atmosphere. Hearty competition.

During that year, while I was sparring, I got my first black eye. I took a bad knock during training and came home with my face a little roughed up, just a tad bloody here and there. My mom was in the living room reading when I got home. Normally you'd expect a mom to leap from her chair, coddling you. "What happened, are you okay? Please go lie down in bed. Is there anything I can get you to make you feel better?" But my mom just looked at me squarely, then looked back at her reading.

I stood there, paused for a while, a little disappointed in her quiet. And she looked back up at me, her face very clear. "Oh don't complain," she said. "You want to be a boxer. This is your price. Don't whine. A boxer gets hit. A boxer gets bloody. Get used to it. This is normal."

And just like that, it was as though she had given me my second real knock.

After a year, and a couple of black eyes, my brother and trainer said it was time for a real fight. I didn't know if I was interested. I'd gotten comfortable with where I was. I enjoyed it and didn't want to mess that up. And truthfully, I was probably a little scared. It's going from ground level and putting yourself on the platform, and any time you try to elevate your game, it can seem daunting. But my trainer took me aside and said something I will never forget.

"You are not a boxer. You are too small, too thin, not nearly powerful enough. But if you follow my advice—if you work hard—your efforts will be repaid. You will be glad you did this."

And so I agreed. I trained for four more months, only slightly more intensely, and then I had my first fight. It was exhilarating being there in that ring. At first you worry about the people watching. You're so cognizant of them. But when you step in and make that first swing, everything else just sort of stops and spins. It's surreal. Unfortunately, I didn't win that first match, but I didn't lose either. We tied. And my character at the time—a rambunctious sixteen-year-old boy mind you, wasn't comfortable with such a verdict, so I told my trainer I wanted to fight again. He set a few things up, and I won the second fight. That, of course, meant I had that sweet taste of victory, so I said, "Again." And the third fight, in natural course, I lost. It was a perfect mixture of average, and if there's anything I hate to be it's average. You are bad or you are great. You are committed or you are not. The murky is a place for nobodies.

After that third fight and a good solid walk thinking about the situation, I went to my trainer's apartment and knocked on his door. "I have to speak with you," I said. "I've been boxing for a year and a half. I've had three fights. I won one, lost one, and tied one. I'm not comfortable with this. Now we will train for real. You will teach me to be a winner or I will stop altogether."

And, standing there on his doorstep, cloaked in that bit of midnight, I think he finally knew what kind of character he had in front of him, and I think I finally realized the kind of character I had, too. I wasn't good at this. I wasn't built for it. Forget a natural superstar. If I was going to do this, I was going to have to put everything I had into it. It would take time; it would take effort. I would lose out on moments with my friends and time for goofing off, but I had my mother's instinct inside me. You decide to do something and you pay the price for it, or you toss it away and move onto something else.

"Fine," he said. "We'll train now a minimum of four to five months to make you better than you are now, and then you'll fight again. But you have to train hard. You have to come in no less than four times a week. You have to run in the mornings. You have to give this everything that you have." And I smiled at this, because everything I had was the least I wanted to give.

After that period of training, I began to win. There was only one loss in my entire boxing career that I regretted, and it was the first one, because it was the only fight where I didn't put my all into it. After that, I lost only eleven times. Nine of those times were before the limit, and my trainer pulled me out of the ring to forfeit. He knew I wasn't a strong boxer, so if I got in the ring and stood no chance of winning—only hurting myself greatly and ruining my career—he'd pull me out. One blow to the head in boxing and you can be done, you know? In a way, it was really a method of survival. But I knew, as he knew, that he had to be the one to make that decision. On my own, I'd never be able to give up.

After that, success seemed to propel me forward at an unlikely rate. When I was twenty-one, I was selected as one of the three boxers to represent Switzerland at the 1976 Olympic Games in Montreal. It was perhaps one of the most surreal moments of my life. I'd been training hard; I'd been fighting, but really only to be as good as I possibly could. I had two Swiss boxing championships under my belt, but I'd never set out to be a part of the Olympic Games. And yet there the opportunity was, sitting on my doorstep, only six years after I'd set foot in a gym.

After I found out that I had been selected, I decided to take four months off from working to concentrate entirely on training. Seven days a week, morn to eve, I'd be focused wholeheartedly on excelling at the sport. It wasn't an easy decision. It's certainly hard to pay the bills, to make ends meet, when you don't have that paycheck coming in. You don't have time to hang out with your friends, have a girlfriend, or travel. You become married to the ring. But I considered those the prices that I had to pay in order to be an Olympic boxer. If you're going to do this, I told myself, you can't do it halfheartedly. And so my trainer and I began rigorously training, working harder than I ever had in my life. It was early mornings. It was late nights. It was sweating and running and bleeding.

Fourteen days before we were scheduled to leave for Montreal, my trainer came and knocked on my door. I remember him standing there in the frame, looking so solemn. The life had been knocked right out of him. I imagined something had happened to his family. He had to have received some terrible news. He was the kind of man who had sun in his eyes every day; I'd never seen him look so dejected. He hung there in the doorway holding a slender, folded envelope. He handed it to me and I read it. He'd received a letter from an official crewmember of the Swiss boxing team.

There was a huge problem with the federation. A scandal really. The current president of the boxing federation at that time had taken all the funds from the account, and due to the nature of the misconduct, the Swiss boxing team could no longer go to the Olympics. He'd been arrested and put in jail. An investigation was underway, the letter assured.

I had never had such a blow in my career.

The investigation was slow. The justice not so swift. I kept my hope up until the day we were scheduled to leave, but we never got the okay, so the plane took off, minus three Olympic athletes.

It was the biggest disappointment I'd had in my life thus far, and it still remains one of the biggest disappointments of my life. I'd done everything I could do, everything I could control, but in the end it didn't matter. The selfish motives of one overtook the hard work of another. That day I learned a hard lesson—one that is still, at times, tricky to swallow. *Sometimes no matter how many things you do right, life has its own course. Try as you might, you cannot control everything.* Suffice it to say, I was glad the president was already in a jail, because if I had seen him on the street, I know I would have punched him in the nose straight away. After that, I told my trainer I was going to quit boxing. I was twenty-one years old. I'd won two championships and suffered one massive disappointment. It was plenty on both ends of the spectrum.

"I can't do this," I told him. "I pushed myself to the maximum and this is what it got me." He looked at me steadily, almost as if he were unsure at first of what to say. But as always, his advice was concise, to the point, and on target.

"You can stop, of course. You're right. I understand your frustration and I understand your decision. I'd probably want to make the same one myself. But one day you will be fifty years old and you will only have one thing on your mind—the regret—because you love being a boxer. And you will never have this chance again."

I took two or three months off to think about it. I was still unsure. But after those few months, I knew he was right. I couldn't quit something I loved because of the failure of another. I couldn't cut the journey short. So I laced my gloves back up and went into the ring for six more years, until I was twenty-seven years old.

In the end, I boxed for twelve years, fought eighty-four fights, won six championships, and learned how to take a few knocks. It was certainly a trait I would need in the coming years.

CHAPTER FOUR

The Mountain Love

"Struggling and suffering are the essence of a life worth living. If you're not pushing yourself beyond the comfort zone, if you're not demanding more from yourself—expanding and learning as you go—you're choosing a numb existence. You're denying yourself an extraordinary trip."

—Dean Karnazes

After I left boxing, the next step was remarkably clear. The place I always felt called to—and felt challenged on—was the side of a mountain. My mother had taught me the love of the mountains as a child, and I knew the kind of man it took to be a master of it—at least as much as a man can ever master such an unwieldy work of God. And one of the world's greatest peaks—the Matterhorn—sat tempting me out of the ring and into the world's backyard. The decision practically made itself.

I've always said to tell the story of the Matterhorn is to tell the story of my life. Even the easiest route up it is already very hard. I say that not, of course, in a complaining way, or in a regretful manner, but rather in thanksgiving. Challenge is the root of everything wonderful I've received in my life.

Technically difficult and physically taxing, the real Matterhorn has a summit of 4,478 meters (14,692 ft.), making it one of the highest, and perhaps the most intricate climb in the Alps. But the scale is small compared to the success of the summit. Swallowing a deep breath high above the town of Zermatt, looking down at the Theodul pass, you understand why it was worth it. You understand why determination is one of the most desirable and advisable qualities of humankind.

But the story does not end with the summit. Tracing your way back to base camp is just as difficult as ascending to the fierce peak. Each year, on average, twelve people take their last breath hanging on to the Matterhorn's icy crevices—most on their way down.

The Matterhorn was one of the last peaks to be conquered, and it would mark the end of the Golden Age of Alpinism. It was July of 1865, when Edward Whymper made the first successful, if not unblemished, ascent. It was not the first time someone had tried to climb the mountain that clung so stiffly on the Swiss-Italian border. Seven failed attempts had already been scratched in the books. But Whymper, with a team of six, had made it to the top—finally! It was a moment of pure elation, but that elation dissipated far too quickly. If only they had all been so lucky, and surefooted, to make it to the bottom.

For three years, from 1862 to 1865, Whymper had been in a battle with John Tyndall, an Irish scientist who likewise had his eye on the formidable peak. The two had been racing, each diligently trying to ascend the mountain via the Italian slopes. But they failed, again and again. Tired of losing the battle, Whymper turned to the Swiss side. It was formidable. Almost taunting in its ferocity. And many believed, as Whymper did, that ascent via the Swiss route would be more deadly than ascent via the Italian side. They were going on looks. Human instinct. The word of the mountaineering world. The irony, of course, is that mountains are rarely confined to human supposition. While the Swiss route might have borne a more menacing, terrifying face, it was indeed more passable. And after a few excursions up the Swiss side, Whymper discovered a path hidden behind a steep rock, and, with his team of six additional men, he beat the Irish Tyndall to the title.

On the way down, though, the story was less victorious. Each man on the team tied himself to the next, hitching the group of seven to one rope. The hope was that in binding them all together, each would be less likely to stumble over the edge. But the camaraderie proved costly. When the lead man on the descent slipped, losing his foothold, the three immediately after him tumbled with him, plummeting down the sharp face of the mountain in deathly screams that clung to the ears of those who remained behind. It was only by a stroke of luck, or grace, that the rope broke between the fourth climber and the fifth. The fracture left three men alive, dangling, all too close to the loss of human life they'd just witnessed. They made it to the bottom, intact with both victory and defeat.

Whymper would go down as a pioneer in the field of mountaineering. He carved out the presence of ingenuity and inventiveness. His ascents were a conversation with the mountain, a dialogue where he could listen to how the imposing piece of nature most wanted to be handled.

In 1871, he published a book, entitled *Scrambles Amongst the Alps,* where he detailed his many adventures in mountaineering, including the notorious summit of the Matterhorn. His feelings then are much like mine now. A reverence, a deep respect, and a perpetual awe for the natural marvel that is the mountain and the small details that grace it—from the precocious wildflowers to the glimmering ice. Despite his enduring love affair with these peaks, he would never again attempt to summit an Alpine peak.

"Climb if you will," he wrote, "but remember that courage and strength are naught without prudence, and that a momentary negligence may destroy the happiness of a lifetime. Do nothing in haste; look well to each step, and from the beginning think what may be the end."

Ultimately, the north face of the Matterhorn—known as one of the great six faces of the Alps—was not conquered until 1931. It remains one of the most deadly peaks. From when it was first climbed by Whymper in 1865 to the year 1995, over five hundred individuals have succumbed to its noble trickery.

When I decided to become a mountain guide at the age of twenty-seven, the Matterhorn was in the back of my mind. To do really well, I need a challenge, something significant to strive for, and I could think of nothing that would be a better test of my physical stamina and mental capacity than to become an expert of the Alps' many faces. The mountains were simply in my blood.

When my mother was young, her mother and father brought her to the mountains near the Matterhorn every summer. From age twelve to sixteen, she'd spent weeks scrambling up the surface of the craggy rocks. In mountaineering, there's a line of accomplishment that begins at 4,000 meters. That's the point where it's work for everyone. An invisible line when you nod your head and say, "Well done." Thirty-eight hundred meters, no one bats an eye. But 4,000 meters, absolutely. That's something. And my mother knew that, too. Even when she was that young. And in Switzerland, we have thirty-seven different peaks over 4,000 meters, which translates to thirty-seven different chances to feel this sense of accomplishment. And so at the mere age of twelve, she completed her first 4,000-meter climb—scaling Allalin (4,027 meters or 13,212 feet) and becoming the youngest woman ever to do so. Sixty years later, when she was seventy-two, my brother, Yves, took her back out to the mountain and guided her to the same summit once more.

And so, that is a bit of what was in my blood when I decided that I needed a change in my life. My boxing career had hit a point where there was no room left to grow, so I sent a letter to the Swiss Boxing Federation telling them my story had come to a close. And that very afternoon I sent in my registration to become a mountain guide candidate. The decision was made just like that, and from that point on, all my effort went toward becoming a guide.

Becoming a mountain guide is not a small thing. It's not a feat you decide on and then casually pick up. You don't go to a career office, fashioned in your best suit and tie, coddling a neatly printed resume, and hope that your charm and decent good looks will make up for your shortcomings. You can't promise to learn on the job. Once you're on the job, it's not a deadline in your hands, or a project... it's a human life. Yours and those of the people you're guiding. And do you know what that's really like? Knowing that if you say, "Go left," people will go left. And if you say, "Go right," people will go right. And at the end of the day it's your choice, your word, your instincts that get mothers and fathers and daughters and husbands home happy and safe with memories that will last a lifetime.

The selection process to become a guide, especially in Switzerland, is pretty demanding. The experience required to even start the training is a competence level so high that many are immediately ineligible. You have to be able to manage any situation on the mountain, no matter how ruined your tools, no matter how inclement the weather, no matter how inexperienced your companions.

The Swiss mountain guide training is the standard all over the world—from America to Canada to France. There are roughly 1,350 qualified guides who are a member of the Swiss Mountain Guides Association, about 1 percent of which are women. You have to be a master at the fundamentals and the details—mountaineering, climbing, trekking, and skiing. You have to be fluent in no less than two languages. You have to be calm and collected, but always vigilant for danger. The mountain is not a tamed thing. It has a personality all its own.

In 1984, when I began the course, it took three years to pass the final mountain guide exam. After the first year, you took an exam to transition from merely being a candidate to being a true aspiring mountain guide. In order to pass this portion, you had to earn a minimum of four points on a number of skills—everything from skiing in any condition and maneuvering through bad weather and fog to mastering the compass, maps, rescue, avalanches, crevices, rock climbing, and ice climbing.

For me, the most difficult part was technical skiing. I only started to ski when I was sixteen years old. Thanks to my mom, I did all the technical mountain climbing from a tiny age, I could find my way in and out of anywhere with a compass, and I could build a feast on the highest ledge, but skiing early on was simply too expensive. So at age sixteen, I sought to learn the art on my own, never taking so much as one hour of lessons. There are many people who are skiers who guide on the mountain, but I've always been just the opposite. I'm a mountain guide with skis. It's an advantage now, I think. But at the time it was quite the obstacle.

When it came time for the first-year exam, one of the teachers pulled me aside and said, "What are we going to do with you, Serge? You are the highest on all levels for nearly all categories, but your skiing...." And there he paused and shook his head, mimicking a disappointed father. "We don't know what to do with you. The minimum score you can receive is four and the maximum is a six, but if we're being honest, you're a 3.5."

This worried me, of course. If you're under the limit and don't pass, you can't move forward and have to try again the next year. And the thought of being held back, well I'm sure you can guess, dear reader, how that weighed on me.

I gave it my best, but I wasn't foolish enough to believe I had passed. When the scores came back, though, remarkably, I had a four. My teacher winked at me. "You have to train hard these next two years, Serge," he said. "You have to be better on the final exam."

I left that day thinking about what my boxing trainer had told me thirteen years ago, as I stood there, barely with a bruise on my knuckles. "You're not a boxer, but you'll be surprised what you can do when you apply yourself." The same applied to skiing. Some talents aren't natural. Some have to be forced into evolution. I knew I was lucky to make it through, and I wouldn't waste the opportunity.

After the first year, 70 percent of the group was cut. Only forty-two of us remained. We were separated into groups of six from there, and we did all of our training and runs together with one expert. You become a close knit team when you end up spending so many nights with the same people, out in the wilderness, breathing thin air and existing at higher altitudes. We all trained hard and passed our final exams. We were official mountain guides.

As I write this, of the six in my group, only two of us are still alive. The rest died on the mountain, picked off over the years in a variety of fashions. The other survivor suffered a close call. He was caught in an avalanche and fully buried—found frostbitten and in a coma. His life was saved by a matter of minutes, if not seconds.

That shows how risky this job is. The best job in the world—but not the easiest.

The truth about being a mountain guide is that most of the time the experience is great and easy. You can't imagine that what you call your profession other people call their holiday. What luck! But then there are those two to three times a year that really scare you. Where you wake up and realize the mountain is a beast on its own terms, and sometimes it just doesn't matter if you're the best guide or if you make great decisions. Sometimes there are no good choices; there's only the whim of nature.

I can distinctly remember four or five times over the past twenty-eight years where it felt like I was staring at the headlights myself. And each time when I got home—because I've always been blessed to come home—I can't help but believe there's got to be some God out there who decided it wasn't my time, because I know it was nothing that I did or said that got me off the mountain.

My first big scare was in my first year as a mountain guide. I'd gone out with one customer to climb a ridge. We'd checked the weather before we left and felt pretty confident. A storm was coming, but it wasn't anticipated until much later in the evening. We'd have plenty of time to get in a full day's climb and slink back to our homes, exhausted and relaxed with a warm meal and sparking fire. I was thankful for the forecast. As a mountain man, you're always at the mercy of the weather as much as the peaks.

The day started well. The man was a decent climber, which made things easier, and the wall was sharp and high. The weather was at a perfect notch, too. Not enough to make you boil and not cold enough to touch your bones. We edged our way up the wall and hit the top of the ridge, feeling satisfied.

But just as we came over the cusp, there was an unpleasant gift, wrapped in knotted clouds and pockets of black darkness. Just clearing through the sky was the beginning of a storm, sitting there poised like a word on the tip of a tongue, just ready to fall out. And it was breaking fast. Even if we hurried, I knew it might catch us on the way back.

I got my customer going again and we were making decent time, but we were following two other climbers—young, teenage boys who were on the ridge alone. My God, they looked scared. Well-built and seemingly strong, each movement they made seemed haphazard and rushed. *They'll make a mistake soon*, I thought. *One they can't take back.* A mountain, after all, is never as forgiving as a person.

Clearly, they felt the same way.

"Can we get on your rope?" they asked panting, their voices hysterical. They had these wide, terribly innocent eyes. I don't think they'd ever been so terrified in their entire lives.

I looked at my customer. I knew what I would do, but in a situation like that, it's not really my choice.

"It's your call," I said. "You paid. If we bring them along on our rope, we're at least twice as slow. The storm will catch us and who knows what it will do with us."

The man, thankfully, was a good one. He didn't hesitate to do the right thing.

"What can we do?" he asked. "We can't leave two teenage boys out here alone. We'll wake up tomorrow morning and read their names in the paper. Two young boys die on a ridge during a storm. No, we can't have that."

And he looked over at the boys' faces that were washed in relief. I brought them over onto our rope and we kept going, albeit much slower.

The storm caught us on the way down while we were repelling— a hard time to be hit, as repelling can be one of the most dangerous parts of climbing. You're reliant entirely on your equipment. Those manmade devices are the only things keeping you from an unpleasant meeting with the ground.

The storm hit in waves. The first pass rained in sheets. Rocks were tossed about like little pieces of confetti. We dangled against the side of the wall, hoping nature would protect us from nature. But that was nothing compared to the second storm. It moved overhead, cloaking the sky in a gray film. The temperature dropped an unbelievable twenty degrees, nearly instantaneously, and the rope guiding us down, which had been so supple, was crusted frozen like a razor wire. I got the three climbers down first and began to follow suit when an incredible thing happened: lightning struck. And then there I was, falling. Falling toward the earth. I couldn't feel it, though. I couldn't feel a thing. The lightning, after all, had struck me.

In what would be the luckiest of events, I had done something I rarely do. I had tied a French Prusik knot for myself. The odd thing about being a mountain guide is that you're always so cautious with your customers. You check every little detail to save them. But when it comes to yourself—either out of self-assuredness or hope for a quicker speed—you don't always do the extra, the little things, extra-well. And one of those things I don't always do is tie the French Prusik knot for myself.

This type of safety knot, which is tied below the rappel device, slides down the rope with you as you go down. It's not necessary for repelling, but it's another safety measure. If you stop mid-rappel, it tightens and keeps you from going down further. With the knot in place, you can let go of the ropes, you can clear snags, it keeps you from losing control, and it stops you if you're hit by something like a falling rock—or lightning.

When I came to, I hung there in the air in shock, and then, very carefully, kept going down with my hands trembling with arthritic shakes the entire time. And that's the shock of the mountain. No matter what happens, no matter how scared you are, you have to keep going. To give up is to greet death with a handshake.

I made it down to the ground inevitably. And when my feet hit the rock, my entire body was convulsing. Shakes of pure disbelief. When you are that close to death and when you escape it, you think you must be lying to yourself. Your life has been forever changed; you now believe in miracles.

We arrived in Chamonix late in the evening, and for all the terror of the day, we were a band of four happy smiles. The young boys were incredibly grateful and promised they would never forget what I had done for them. And indeed they were telling the truth. Even though it's been such a long time now, decades really, every year those boys—now men—write me a letter to thank me for saving their lives.

It's amazing how memories like that can stick in your mind, how one close encounter with death is like a trigger point that's hit every time you're on the border of safety. There was a time, years later, when I was doing a climb on the north face of the Matterhorn, and the image of those boys stuck in my head again. I was out alone on the mountain doing a solo climb, which is really the maximum risk for everybody. You've got no rope, no people, no nothing. You make one mistake, and you fall down, meters and meters, to your death. But to me, that's always been a bit of security. When you know you can't make a mistake, your attention is so taut, so focused, that you're the safest that you ever are on the mountain. You don't have to worry about someone else goofing up or making a wrong move. You're reliant entirely on your own skills, and to me that's a relief.

When I solo climb, I always choose something two levels under my highest skill level. That provides a sort of balance and safety net in case something wrong happens. At least then I have the comfort of knowing that I'm within my range of expertise. But when I was out that day, no amount of expertise really mattered.

It was beautiful weather. The sun was cresting right over the mountain. You could tell spring was on its way and that the flowers were aching to burst forth. I was getting in one last climb before all the snow melted. It was one of those moments that was supremely perfect. There I was, all alone, a solitary figure on a mountainside. It was a challenging route, just enough to get my heart rate up and keep my drive happy, but it was leisurely enough to where I didn't have to press myself if I didn't want to. I did half of the face in a very nice time and was feeling pleased with myself, when all of a sudden, just like a snap of a twig, I was hanging onto the face by only a single ice pick.

The sun apparently had been gnawing at the ice all morning and a grapefruit-sized rock had wiggled its way out of the mountain's hold. And in a matter of seconds—as I'd been gloating about my glorious day—it fell and plunked me right over the kneecap. And we're not talking about a subtle touch here. Not like someone tapping you on the shoulder and asking politely if they could squeeze on through. No, the force of the rock that was travelling somewhere between the speed of really fast and oh-my-God fast, was powerful enough to knock me off my holds. I lost one ice pick and one crampon and hung there, stranded. The isolation on the mountain that had, just moments before, been so incredibly invigorating, was all of a sudden, downright terrifying. One second I was climbing confidently, and the next I was hanging like a clown.

I started shaking badly. And I remembered, just like that, the faces of those boys when we'd been climbing before. How did we make it down then? And how would I make it down now with solely one ice pick and one crampon?

I stayed half an hour in that exact position, learning to breathe slowly again, convincing myself that I hadn't died and that I could get back to base camp in one piece. And then I came all the way down, gradually, painstakingly. Miraculously, really.

When I got home that night, still with a bit of the shakes, to be honest, I walked out into the backyard to see my kids, Clara and Steve, jumping over logs. They were just young things then. Incredibly tiny lives that were blooming. They had no idea they'd almost lost their dad that day.

I took a deep swallow and walked inside. My mother had always told me that you pay the price for your dreams, and I knew she was right. But it was starting to look more and more like the price for mine would be my life.

The World Tour Begins—February 13, 2000

Leaving little Switzerland to run the big, wide world.

Passports—"keys" for border crossings on World Tour by the romantic couple!

The World Tour

African kids loved to run with Nicole.

Crossing the Mekong River.

Nicole on motorcycle—not all roads are paved on the World Tour.

Meet Nicole and Her Parents

Out on the town.

The beauty with the sparkling eyes.

Nicole's parents visit in South Africa during the World Tour.

The young beauty strolling.

Nicole recording the joys and sorrows of the day in her diary.

Meet Serge's Family

With his influential mother—stern, yet loving.

What do we play next?

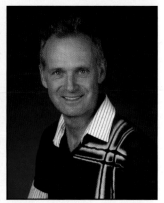

Serge—the fascinating story teller/motivational speaker.

Nora loved the mountains—a legacy bequeathed to her sons.

Meet Serge's Family

Serge with his children, Clara and Steve.

Magic of the Christmas fire in a special cave.

Serge with first grandchild; he now has two.

Clara and husband with Serge's first grandchild.

Serge and His Family

Serge with his children, Clara and Steve.

Serge's first wife with their children, Clara and Steve.

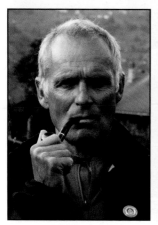

Serge and his pipe—his one luxury item on the World Tour.

Clara and Steve visiting in Agadir, Morocco.

Meet Serge and Nicole—the 25,000 Mile Love Story Couple

A tender moment.

A humorous moment.

Together around the world—one of many lonely days on the road.

A fond moment in the vineyards where Nicole grew up.

Paying the Price

Serge in water rehab from 1986 knee surgery—screws still in knee during World Tour.

Serge recovering from a broken ankle in 1984.

A pup tent as home, sweet home for over 1200 nights on the World Tour.

Serge survived macheteing his way through The Darien Gap—most dangerous area in the world.

Serge, the Mountain Guide

Serge on the mountaintop—beauty after the quest.

The Mountain Guide Building—home of an elite mountain guide school.

Mountain guide again after the World Tour.

Serge on the mountain—where he is most at home.

Serge, the Endurance Athlete

The boxer–six time Swiss lightweight champion.

The Climber—skill was helpful in reaching apex of highest mountains of 4 continents.

The Rower—rowed Atlantic Ocean with Ole Elmer in 63 days—Canary Islands to Barbados.

The bicyclist—11,200 miles across North America.

Serge, the Endurance Runner

Ran the Pan American Highway—longest road in the world.

Nike Long Run—Palermo to Milano—1,100 miles in 41 days.

American Challenge completed in Fairbanks—14,984 miles run.

Gibraltar to Cape North, Norway—4,359 miles.

Honors and Awards

Serge with his boxing trophies.

*1976 Swiss Olympic Boxing Team—
no official defeats, just one huge
disappointment!*

*Treasured drawing from teen in
Lebanese jail.*

Publicity for the American Challenge and the World Tour

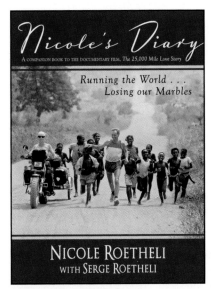

Cover of Nicole's Diary.

2005 Time Europe cover—Serge & Nicole among 37 European heroes and photo of Serge with many pairs of running shoes.

Cover of the American Challenge book.

Humanitarian efforts of the American Challenge through the François-Xavier Bagnoud Foundation.

Partnership with
International Vision Quest—Helping the Poor

Nicole, Serge, Dr. Ron Zamber and Susan Zamber with IVQ sign.

Every little drop helps!

Serge, Dr. Zamber, and child they assisted in Costa Rica.

Nicole checking child's eyes with new glasses—I can see!

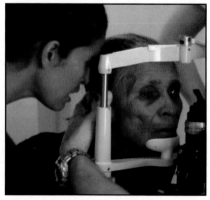

IVQ eye examination—helping the poor in Costa Rica.

Running the World to Help Kids

Third-world kids provide Serge more "fuel" for running.

Serge and Nicole showing their love for kids and vice versa.

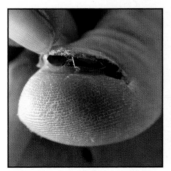

Serge loses a toenail running for kids.

One more hour without medical help and Serge would have been dead.

Running to Raise Awareness of the Plight of Children in Poverty

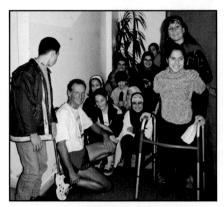

Poverty-stricken Middle Eastern children.

A lonely, impoverished South American child.

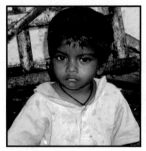

Viewing poverty firsthand is so heart-wrenching.

Nicole with kids—her heart goes out to poverty-stricken kids.

Poverty and its impact on children.

CHAPTER FIVE

Nicole Number Two

"Once upon a time there was a boy who loved a girl, and her laughter was a question he wanted to spend his whole life answering."
—Nicole Krauss

I wasn't looking for her, but there she was. An uncanny spirit spilling out into the room. Her green eyes danced, catching flecks of light and a bit of laughter. The kind that is so genuine you lose your breath a little. She had this brown hair, just a tad mossy and unkempt, but that swept up bits of gold as she moved her head from side to side, talking and drawing her glass of wine up to her mouth. She was remarkably young. And light. A fleeting moment that kept coming back, not unlike a carousel.

The Mocambo Café and Bar sat on the Rue de la Dent-Blanche, huddled into the center of Sion. A tavern that wasn't particularly extraordinary. You wouldn't notice it if you were walking by and you wouldn't remember it when you left, unless, of course, you happened across something there that was remarkable. The place itself had a very barebones expression with tawny walls that were worn down and covered in fake Japanese art and amateur paintings. The furnishings were minimal. It was thrown together as if someone had discovered all the odds and ends from a grandmother's basement and then let them wreak havoc above ground.

She was sitting at the table with a young man, only slightly older by his looks. I'd met him once or twice before. A good guy by any standards who had a tenderness in his voice. And he liked her, of course. You could tell by the way he bent his head and how his body leaned just ever so slightly toward hers when he'd pick up his heavy glass of merlot, slosh it around the dial of the glass, and then take a thoughtful swallow. But I didn't think much of it. There are types of people everyone likes and this girl, the girl with the brunette hair, was bound to be one of them.

I was there that day with one of my clients. We were talking about a climb he wanted to do. He had asked me to lead him, but I was leaving that very week to do a seven-month run, so this climb would have to wait. Today we were merely talking through the details. Biting his fingernails, he was unsure if he could make it. What would the weather be like? How long would it take? I tried to give him my best attention, reassuring him, but what can I say? Someone else was distracting me.

My heart didn't take long. Gut feelings are uncomplicated like that. Instinctual. There are expressions you can share with any human being. Passing glances that go unnoticed. But some people you can look at and know immediately that you will never again look that way at anyone else. One simple glance at her and my blood was pumping. It rushed over my body, from my sturdy ankles to the roots of my hair. It feels a bit like sandpaper to say love at first sight. That saying can seem too enchanted. I mean, how can that much magic exist in so much reality? But sometimes you can't get around it.

Sometimes magic is the only thing that makes sense.

Once my client left, I walked across the width of the hardwood floors, the oak bending beneath my steps, my feet not quite keeping up with my mind. I learned when I was young that when you find something or someone that takes your heart up a floor, you don't pause. When you hesitate, you lose things.

I was so very aware of every notch in my stomach, every buckle in my knees. I hadn't been nervous in years, but there was something about this woman who was so small in build and yet so large in presence that gave my normal sensibilities the unpredictability of a tumbleweed. I stopped beside their table, taking her in for a minute, before grabbing hold of the back of a rickety chair and saying, "May I sit here with you?" and then promptly sliding myself in—not allowing for the possibility that the answer could ever be no.

People throughout your entire life will tell you to be practical. They will pack into your brain the belief that you should be as sensible and well-rounded as a sturdy sedan. They will tell you that you can't do certain things, that certain things are impossible. They will want you to find a partner that softens your instincts to be brash, to run naked in the streets, to have one too many. *Be reasonable*, they'll cry. *At some point you have to act like an adult.* And these people aren't bad. They're just a little too molded. So plucked of their feathers that they can't remember they're birds—creatures that can fly so miraculously high and far that the clouds themselves become the size of raisins.

The absolute beauty of meeting someone new is that up until that point your lives have been on entirely different trajectories. You have laced up your shoes in different homes and bowed your head to different family prayers. You have awakened under different sides of the sun and broken bread with a thousand different people. But all those decisions and experiences—no matter how different they might be—have led you to a remarkable point of sameness where your feet are standing on the same pavement and you can shake hands in the same room, in the same time zone, in the same moment.

I got the feeling as I sat at the table that Nicole was very much a horse on the starting blocks. She was just so powerful, ready to be set free. She had this energy that had been bottled up in her for years that she needed to let loose in some direction. She was ready to change her life. I suppose it could have been with a painter in New York or with a chef in France. Knowing her now, knowing what we've been through, I imagine she would have been willing to go with anyone. But I got to her first. And so she wouldn't change her life by painting or cooking or teaching. She would change it by running.

She was only twenty-one, thirteen years my junior, but she was remarkably mature. She grew up in Ardon, a small village only six or so miles from Sion. When she was a young child, she was a rather plump little girl, already very energetic. She had parents who loved her enough to show her the true value of life—the virtues of hard work, honesty, and independence. Everything she had came from effort and self-will. From a young age, she was out on the mountainside working in the vineyards. In Ardon, the hillsides are steep. They stick up like ladders, climbing with the vines to well above 2,400 feet. She never went camping, but she was familiar with the outdoors and enjoyed spending time in the vineyards, the forest, and having enormous picnics with her parents.

Her mother—typically a very active, energetic woman, typically beside her in the fields—began suffering from bouts of pain when Nicole was still very small. She would find herself busy around the house, doing something as simple as ironing a shirt, when a pain so sudden and intense would shoot through her, immobilizing her. Over time, the pain spread, causing inflammation, and it wasn't long before the disease took over, destroying much of the cartilage and bone within her joints. The muscles, ligaments, and tendons, which normally so stably frame the joints, weakened. It wasn't long after that, that Nicole's mother was confined to her bed. The arthritis had progressed to such a stage that simple tasks such as filling up a water kettle or hanging up the laundry were not only difficult but also impossible.

In the midst of her mother's illness, Nicole encountered her own difficulties. Walking through town one day, a reckless driver ran into her, sending her skidding through the air and landing, with a great thump, upon the grass. For three straight months after the accident, her world was in a heavy fog. The doctors called it a cerebral concussion and promised it would just take a little time before she was back up to her full speed and running once again.

But after healing up, just a few short years later, Nicole was working in a cosmetics factory in Chateauneuf where she was on the factory line. The health gods were against her and she suffered a severe bout of chemical poisoning. The episode spiraled and had grave consequences for the growing girl. She had severe burning sensations in her face. She lost her memory, had spells of unconsciousness and amnesia, and found herself frequently falling asleep while on her job. The doctors crowded around her with their stethoscopes and shiny machines and came to a damaging conclusion: cerebral edema.

Cerebral edema is a fancy term for brain swelling. More fluid is found in the skull than there should be, and as a result, the brain balloons. The swelling, of course, has its costs: it can harm the blood flow to the brain or shift the brain around in the skull, causing brain damage or even—if you can imagine it—more fatal consequences. Nicole spent two years of her adolescence trying to return to a healthy equilibrium, suffering through extensive physical and emotional pain.

It's not uncommon that difficulty makes us thankful for brightness, that it makes the risks seem just a little more worthwhile. By the time she got her head back above water, Nicole had a new perspective, one framed by her numerous experiences with the basic value of health. She learned, at a dear cost, that nothing is more precious in the world than our ability to stand on our own two feet, to take in the day through unclouded eyes, to earn our own way, strike our own bargains, and raise our own families. Nicole still reeled from occasional pockets of sickness, but she decided to live in such a manner of thankfulness that she would never close out a day thinking she had not taken full advantage of it. Perhaps she was not prepared for a tremendous adventure. She was a bit green. But I could tell she easily caught the attitudes of those around her, and she had a deep desire to prove others wrong.

When she was young, people would say, "But Nicole will never succeed. It's impossible, coming from a small town. She will never make it." But it was always in her depths that she was a great adventurer. She just had to find it. No matter what, she would always be joyful, thrilled, and blessed. And that was the woman who then sat across from me. I could see it on her face. It was contagious. The fibers of sheer gratitude and understanding.

Nicole had been working as a waitress at the Mocambo for two years. When business was slow, the owner, Madeleine, would let Nicole join friends, partaking in a deep cabernet or pensive merlot. The boy with her was Charles-Henri, an affable fellow who drank and smiled and didn't seem to mind my boldness at all. He talked some at first, but his presence sort of wilted away as Nicole and I settled into what would become our language. A hilarious, comfortable, intoxicating dialogue of light touches, energetic laughs, and meaningful words. Like an adolescent schoolboy, I was determined that she would be mine.

I left that week for Gibraltar and then spent seven months running. Running from Gibraltar in a northerly direction across Europe all the way to North Cape on the Artic coast of Norway, a distance of 7,015 kilometers (4,359 miles). After returning home to Sion and my job as a mountain guide, I stopped one day at the Mocambo for a cup of coffee. The waitress with the twinkling green eyes was still there, causing a certain electricity in the air. Madeleine, the owner of the Mocambo, and I were old friends. They weren't very busy that day, so she had time to chat about my trek. The waitress joined us, as I described the arduous run. When Madeleine inquired about Nicole Sauthier, the mother of my two children, I had to admit that we had decided to separate. She and the children had accompanied me in a camper on the European run, and we had come to the mutual decision that our relationship was no longer working.

December arrived with all the gaiety of the approaching holiday. Shortly before Christmas, I returned to the Mocambo with Danièle, the warden of a mountain cabin that I still frequently use on alpine treks with clients. The coffee was excellent, but the real treat was watching the wine waitress. There were these secretive glances with a strange intensity. Danièle noticed them, too, and wasn't very happy. Finally I shouted: "I will come back here for the eyes of the wine waitress."

I was, however, a bit bashful about the return. After all, how was I to know if her heart was taken or if it could be taken by me, so I purchased a bouquet of flowers so huge that they covered my face. Maybe she would be so pleased by them, I reasoned, that she wouldn't care who was carrying them. And promptly at the stroke of nine, on January 2, 1991, I entered the busy Mocambo, placed the flowers on the counter in front of Nicole, saying only "These are for you," and then taking a seat at a table.

Suddenly, my trips to the Mocambo became more frequent. Every day I had a thirst for coffee. I just liked to watch her, say hello, make a game of it to make her smile. But as I kept coming day by day, I noticed there was another fellow there, too. He was a handsome man, younger than me with thick dark hair. He'd smile at Nicole, too, but his gaze was a bit more bashful.

This worried me. Perhaps she would like him more? Perhaps she would think he was more attractive or kinder? So I did what any man in his right mind would do. I removed the competition.

"Excuse me, sir," I said, "I can't help but notice you've been coming around here a lot lately."

He smiled sheepishly and nodded.

"Well, I just want us to stay on good footing here. You see that woman over there?" And I nodded toward Nicole who was up at the bar, preparing a few glasses of wine for some young women.

He nodded, his smile growing wider by the thought of her.

"Well," I said. "I don't want to have any problems so you should know she is my woman and I don't want anyone else eyeing her. What do we say I pay for your coffee today and you never come back?"

The poor boy was horror-stricken and terribly embarrassed. He gathered his things as quickly as possible, apologizing all the way. I put money on the table for his coffee and chuckled to myself as I sat down waiting for my future wife to say hello.

CHAPTER SIX

You Tell Yourself Forever

"*The meeting of two personalities is like the contact of two chemical substances: if there is any reaction, both are transformed.*"

—C.J. Jung

My life has been a love story. And in so many ways, it's been a perfect one. But not with whom you think and not for the reasons you might think.

When you get married, you tell yourself *forever* because that's what you want to believe. And because at that moment, forever seems possible. You're a little naïve of course. Even if you're forty or fifty, you're still naïve because gosh, it's love. And love makes everyone a little less sensible. You're caught up in the beauty of that woman before you. The one who has curves and glistens and kisses like in a Marilyn Monroe film. You're not thinking then about all of the hard things and the real parts of life. You're not thinking about what could spoil such perfection. And who can blame you or deprive you of such an instinctively flawless feeling? You're just in the moment.

And you can't possibly realize how common it is to fall in love. And how it's just as common to fall out of love.

I've always said that my true lifelong love is nature, and that a woman is the most beautiful piece of it. My parents were married for their whole lives, never breaking their vows until my dad passed away. It was this thin, continuous line of love. It wasn't pretty sometimes. And it wasn't animated. But it was unbroken.

For my part though, I've had the opposite kind of luck. For me, love has been brutally strong and truly animated, but it never really did keep and I, for one, couldn't stick it out when I knew that we were running on borrowed time and memories. In the end, I think, I was just a little too strong for love. But that never kept me from trying.

My first love was Nicole Sauthier. We were partners for fifteen years. We met when we were very young; I was still boxing then. And one night when I was feeling rather down and out, frustrated with my progress, I commenced to stroll the streets. It was really pretty late, probably eleven or so in the evening, and I came across two girls, both with kind, affectionate faces, though there was one I found particularly beautiful. We all got to chatting and spent a healthy portion of the evening walking up and down the streets. Inevitably, the girl I found so interesting had to go, which left me standing across from my second choice. She was a slight thing, perhaps not as pretty as the other girl, but we went to her house and ate some ice cream and talked until the sun rose the next day. She was so quiet, such a kind, gentle spirit, and the way she crossed her legs and smiled at me brought me a sense of peace that was unforgettable. Her gentleness was what I needed then.

We had a number of good years and a number of average ones. There were no big fights, no big blowouts. And that was the problem. There was nothing big at all. It was a constant unruffled sea that sat idly washing waves onto the shore. I had dreams and to her that was fine, but she didn't really have any of her own. She would be entirely content to spend day after day looking out the window.

In the end, we both knew our compatibility had expired. I had a fire under me, an urgency, and she had a knitting needle. We decided it was best for both of us to part ways and we ended our partnership, blessed with two children and the clarity to move forward. When I call her now and again to catch up, her voice is so quiet, so mouse-like, I imagine I must have overwhelmed her all those years.

I met Nicole Gaillard at the Mocambo Café and Bar. I know, it's confusing. You'd think I would have made it easy on you by at least finding a woman with a different name! But, it was to be Nicole again. But this Nicole, she was so very different. To rile her up, I'd always call her Nicole Number Two. She hated that. Her face would go lean and narrow and she'd scoff. She had such a high-spirited personality. When she did something, she threw her whole self into it. She could be loud and brash and temperamental, but with just as much force, she could be generous and loving. With the same amount of passion she used to wound you, she could heal you.

I fell for her hard and fast and strong, and within a week, we were talking about how we could radically change our lives. Do you know what it's like to put two individuals in a room together who are like fireworks at their core? They feed off of each other, spark after spark after spark. It's one intense moment followed by the next, a marathon always. This is a woman I can grow old with, I told myself. This is a woman I can get lost in the world with.

Hadn't I had that thought once before?

CHAPTER SEVEN

The Adventure Begins

"Defeat is not the worst of failures. Not to have tried is the true failure."

—George Edward Woodberry

It would be an injustice to say that Nicole did not change my life, and I hers. After we met, there was a drastic change, a 180 if you will. For me, I had always been pushing myself and testing my boundaries, but what Nicole and I would set out to conquer was on such a grand scale that it could not help but alter my whole world.

In Part II of this book, I will share a collection of stories with you from my time running around the world. Starting in January, 1995, Nicole and I began our decade of running. Over the course of ten years, we would complete the American Challenge, where I ran from Tierra del Fuego—the southernmost tip of Argentina—to Fairbanks, Alaska (almost 15,000 miles in three years) and the World Tour, where I ran 25,422 miles in five years and three months, a distance greater than the circumference of the planet.

While it's impossible to share the entirety of my journeys with you, taking you with me on every stride, these snapshots from my journeys will show you a glimpse of the magic and what it's like to live on the streets and roads of the world, making its inhabitants your neighbors and family, its sidewalks and roadsides your quarters.

But these stories, at least for me, are not only of culture and landscape—though those are vitally important! They are of personal character and achievement and the will to survive, along with a love for adventure, nature, achievement, children, and, of course, a love for Nicole who was at my side on her motorcycle.

The truth is, all the time you are preparing for who you will become. Your experiences multiply to provide you with the character, strength, and endurance to do the unthinkable. From the second I came into this world onto the hospital's sidewalk, I was gearing up for the moment I would take to the roads and truly make them my home. I was preparing myself to rid the world of the impossible.

PART TWO

The Road

CHAPTER EIGHT

The Magic Line

"Nothing behind me, everything ahead of me, as is ever so on the road."

—Jack Kerouac

It all began with a simple question: why not?

And the answer led to a thousand things I never would have expected—eight years of my life on foreign soil, literally running around the world, a marathon every other day. It seemed just as soon as the words were out of my mouth, with the simple prod of "why not," I was darting through white cotton sand and over charcoal asphalt. I was breaking bread with women in the Middle East who were cloaked from the roots of their hair to their ankles. In the Swiss Embassy in Africa, I was watching a war unfold on the lawn, hearing gunshots and bombs ricochet right outside my window. In India, I was sleeping in the same room as twenty other people, everyone piled on top of one another like a stack of cards. And in the Atacama Desert, I was swapping stories with a man who had never seen rain.

And these things, these snippets, they were just the beginning. What in the world had I gotten myself into?

There are many ways to travel, but for the most part there is the easy way, and then there's the real way. When you're out there in the real heart of each continent and not just checking into every five star hotel you come across—taking an air-conditioned tour bus out at noon to "see the sights"—you begin to realize how varied the world really is. How many different languages and how many different customs are puzzled together across the globe. You pick up on the idiosyncrasies, like how looking someone in the eyes in one country is respectful, while in another country it's considered rude. If you're really out there in the thick of it, you realize how much your rules don't matter and how important it is to see and understand how others choose to live their lives. Understanding isn't just a kindness; it's a means of survival. On the road, anything—and I do mean anything—can happen.

I have been an adventurer all of my life. And I know it's not the thing for everyone. It's a way of living for people who are a touch mad and wholeheartedly committed. People think explorers are flighty, bouncing from one spot to the next as though they can't put down roots. But choosing that mobility, that life without comfort or home, that's a commitment in itself.

When Nicole and I were on the road, we ran across a thousand travelers. So many single men strapped tightly into their backpacks. There were a few groups here and there of friends vagabonding across the back roads, and just the occasional solitary woman with her rucksack, looking weathered but fulfilled. Yet, despite the passing years and the miles covered, only once did we come across another married couple exploring the world together, a Parisian couple we met in South Africa who were walking to Jerusalem. At first I thought the lack of couples was curious. What could possibly be better to share with the one you love? But as time went on, it was easy to tell how the road rubs you raw. It shows your true colors in such a relentless way that you still stand naked even when you have all your clothes on. I can't say this enough: The road is a rich way of life, but it's very hard. You give up so much by going.

While this is a collection of stories about the American Challenge and the World Tour, I've been doing things people raised their eyebrows at my whole life. Adventuring was bred straight into me, along with my tiny build and my blonde hair.

The 25,000 Mile Love Story

In 1986, I ran across both Death Valley and the Grand Canyon, trudging the 5,250 feet of descent from the rim of the canyon to the Colorado River, and then running straight back up to the rim again in a single day. In 1989, I took 219 days to run from Gibraltar to Cape North—the northernmost point in Norway—a total of 6,500 miles, averaging 29.7 miles per day. Over the years, I climbed the highest peaks of four different continents: Mt. McKinley in North America, Mt. Aconcagua in South America, Mt. Kilimanjaro in Africa, and Mt. Blanc in Europe.

In the Nike Long Run, I ran from Palermo to Milano, Italy in forty-one days. In Nepal, I ran a 150-mile route through the Himalayan Mountains. Running the Annapurna Circle meant slogging up and down peaks over the course of seven days, with the highest elevation being the Thorong La Pass at 17,589 feet.

I took nine months to bicycle across North America, starting in Montreal and ending up in Florida, covering 11,200 zigzagging miles. And I kayaked the treacherous Nahanni River in the Northwest Territory of Canada, which is aptly nicknamed "the man-eater."

I can't prove these things to you, of course. I didn't have a camera following me around, or a support staff trailing at my heels with Band-Aids and Gatorade. I didn't do these trips for the accolades, for the press, or even for the stories. I did them because I feel more at home hanging on the side of a mountain than I do sleeping in my own bed. And I really believe that if you're not doing what you love in life—no matter what it is—you don't really have much of a life to speak of.

There are plenty of people who hear the things I've done and they say, "You're crazy. Why would you ever want to do that?" Or they listen to me quietly, nodding their heads as if in earnest, but all the while they've decided I'm a fraud, a great exaggerator. But these people don't bother me. You have to expect them. The world is in no shortage of doubters. And they're easier to take, because there are also those whose eyes open up wide, and they lean in to listen a little more closely as I tell them about the time a snake bit straight through my eyelid. Or the time I spent the day in a Lebanese prison. And it's those people who, like me, understand the call of the road. They get it that adventure is something you do because it's the way you feel most alive.

The American Challenge was a new birth for so many reasons. For one, the scale of it was tremendous. The idea, in very broad terms, was that I would run the length of the Pan-American Highway (the longest road in the world) from Tierra del Fuego all the way up to Fairbanks, Alaska. Nicole would peddle her bike beside me, towing or pulling a small trailer. It would take us three years to cover roughly 15,000 miles.

Many people found the idea laughable. I would talk to men and women sitting in the coffee shops, sipping on their espresso, while they politely folded their newspapers to hear me out. I would draw out our route on a paper napkin, explaining how the Pan American Highway would become our home. How we would eat, sleep, and drink of the world's greatest road. And they would look at me as though the best thing they could possibly offer me was a straitjacket. They would sooner believe a man could lasso the moon than spend three years of his life running. In fact, when I contacted a shoe company to sponsor me on the American Challenge, they simply replied that they would not sponsor a mission of death, which was what I was talking about embarking upon.

But the American Challenge was notable for more than its length. On this trip, I wouldn't be alone. I would be going with my wife, Nicole. My previous life partner was such a quiet spirit. She was tender and malleable, incredibly kind and good hearted. She let me do what I wanted, and she loved me through it all. And she blessed me, of course, with our two precious kids. But our relationship was too passive. I didn't need someone following me; I needed someone by my side. I needed someone who had this thirst for life just as much as I did. And from the moment I met Nicole in that cafe, I knew there wasn't a quiet bone in her body. She would not sit idly by, thumbing her fingers; she would truly be a partner.

The remarkable thing looking back on it now is just how eager Nicole was to flip a switch and sign on to such an extreme adventure. She'd never so much as camped out one day in her life. She hadn't built a fire or slept in a sleeping bag. She'd never driven a motorcycle. She only spoke French. Her world was so refined and limited. But without hesitation, she said yes. Three years on the road, camping out all the time, eating only tuna and pasta with tomato sauce. Of course! Sign me up! How many women do you know who would say that?

The 25,000 Mile Love Story

The idea for the challenge itself happened in a rather roundabout manner. It wasn't in our heads at first to run the Pan American Highway. That came later. Nicole and I simply had decided we wanted to do something large and daring together, something to change the course of our lives. And it occurred to us as we were thumbing through our ideas that perhaps we could not only change our lives, but that we could also change the lives of others as well. What if, for example, we could do something to raise money and awareness for impoverished children in the process? Children, after all, represent our future, and they are the most beautiful poetry for which to run. That would make this a real opportunity.

We'd never before attempted anything of this scale. It was a blank slate. But we knew a few things, primarily that no matter how great and pure our intention, money was a key component. We would need to get sponsors. And in order to get sponsors, we'd have to attempt something so radical and unusual that people couldn't help but pay attention.

Nicole and I pulled out a map and unfolded it on our kitchen table. I drew a line from Mexico to Fairbanks, Alaska, and told her this was our best choice. I would run and she would peddle beside me on her bike. Nicole studied the map, tracing her finger along the path we would take. It was about 10,000 kilometers, certainly a worthy challenge. But she looked at it and then back at me with a marked glance of disappointment.

"It's no good," she said, and she—the woman who had never camped a day in her life—pointed straight to the bottom of the map, to Tierra del Fuego. "We do it all or we do nothing."

At that moment it was easy to remember why I married her.

Over the coming months, we debated details. We decided that this was such a large decision that we couldn't rush into it impulsively. We gave ourselves three months to think through the details and make a final decision.

We tried to imagine every possible scenario that could befall us, everything that would prevent us from meeting our goal. People think all adventurers are impulsive, lacking prudence or intentionality. But in truth, the people who lead such risky lives can often be the most careful. Their life depends on it. We knew each detail would need to be hammered out. We'd have to consider health risks, food, and physical danger. There were a myriad of logistics. The whole thing seemed senseless. Overwhelming. And yet . . . it was possible.

After our deliberation period had elapsed, Nicole and I returned to the dining room table. We spread the map back out on the table. It had seen some wear and tear over the past few months as we'd folded it and unfolded it repeatedly, tracing our potential future. This time we stared at it carefully, much like a mother seeing her child's heartbeat for the first time. It's that shocking feeling that what was once just an idea – just a hope – would really actually happen.

The decision was easy. Neither of us hesitated. Yes, we would do the American Challenge. We would start in Ushuai, Argentina, on the southernmost coast of Tierra del Fuego, and we'd travel all the way to Fairbanks, Alaska on our magic line. We'd run and bike 14,984 miles, and, no matter what, we'd never give up. We made a toast that night to the *Desafío Americano*, a nickname given to our new journey. Our goal was to leave in just a matter of months.

That moment, I remember, felt very light and victorious. The decision itself was freeing, as though a load had been lifted from my shoulders. I was flooded with the potential of everything we could accomplish, and I was certain others would feel the contagious spirit, too.

The very next day, I began contacting humanitarian organizations to set up sponsorships. I rambled on and on, peppering people with my excitement. I admit I was a bit naïve. I thought everyone would be clamoring to be a part of this. What a great story! What a great mission! But in the business world, people respond far more quickly to numbers than to the heart.

We sent out press packets to businesses all over the world. In detail, we described our intention and the route we would take. But the responses came back lacking much sentimentality. There is far too much risk, they said. To put everything on one person? What if that one person failed? And it's such a long period of time. Really, it's impossible to support.

Our departure date was delayed multiple times, pushing back month after month, then a year. I had to wonder, does anyone have enough intestinal fortitude these days to be part of such an adventure?

I went off by myself a lot during that period. I'd go to the mountain or to the forest and try to find new ways to keep the lifeblood going. And inevitably Nicole and I decided we couldn't rely on the people with the deep pockets. If this was going to happen, it was going to happen because of the people with the deep hearts. Rather than getting one or two big sponsorships, we sought out to get hundreds. We contacted friends and small business owners. We put advertisements in the paper. We talked and we begged and we prayed people would understand that dreams are worth fulfilling and that a little bit really does go a long way.

When you want to do something that's never been done before, people call it impossible. They shake their fingers and give every excuse in the book. But if you persist long enough, and if you believe firmly enough in what you're trying to accomplish, you'll live long enough to hear someone say yes. And that word will be the sweetest word you've ever heard.

The finances did come into play. And once those were set, we started preparing our equipment. We stripped everything down to bare necessities. We'd leave with a bicycle and a very small trailer, which would house our required provisions: a tent, sleeping bags, a kettle, a coffee pot, two bowls, a press book, a first aid kit, basic tools for repairing the bike, and standard food supply. We'd have two pairs of shoes for me and a change of clothes at all times. Every four to six weeks, we'd stop in a new city to pick up a package with new running gear. The only things we carried that weren't necessary were my pipe, Nicole's make-up kit, and a small object, a sort of talisman. Nicole and I carried it with us everywhere we traveled, while my children, Clara and Steve, had a matching one halfway around the world.

We left Switzerland on January 2, 1995. Our flight to Ushuai took forty-five hours, carting us across the world with stopovers and transfers, but it delivered us safely—if not already slightly exhausted—to the southernmost city of the world. We gave ourselves a few days rest and time to put together last minute logistics, and then, on January 10, our journey truly began. It would take us thirty-five months of effort to cover 24,115 kilometers (14,984 miles), the equivalent of 575 marathons, but we would see it through to Alaska.

CHAPTER NINE

Small World

"We are all strangers in a strange land, longing for home, but not quite knowing what or where home is. We glimpse it sometimes in our dreams, or as we turn a corner, and suddenly there is a strange, sweet familiarity that vanishes almost as soon as it comes."

—Madeleine L'Engle

After months of financial and administrative hair-splitting, we were on the road. First stop Ushuaia, the southernmost portion of Argentina. But the first fluke happened upon landing. Our gear didn't arrive with us. It was lost somewhere between London, Buenos Aires, and Rio Gallegos. They assured us there was no need to panic. It would be there in two days. This set a precedent that would never halt—not during the American Challenge nor during the World Tour. There is no "hurry up" on the road. You can't depend on efficiency. The best thing to do is to learn patience.

We made use of the extra couple of days to hole up in a hotel and write to the people we love—our children, our friends. We did some training in Lapataïa Park, too, located twenty-two kilometers [fourteen miles] south of Ushuaia, where you can see a sign with the words *fin del mundo* [end of the world]. What a piece of truth. The penguins made us think of Antarctica. How close we really were to the tip!

We spent the early evenings walking through the town and, in the midst of the dusty pavement, a worker came running out of a random store one night. "Is there a Serge Roetheli here?" he called. "I have a phone call for him."

It was truly amazing. Someone from home was trying to get in touch with us and, can you imagine, found us in the midst of the streets. Before we'd even left, we realized that we would never be that far from home. What a true relief.

After three days, we finally began the run. That first day, fifty-seven kilometers (thirty-five miles) separated us from our first stopping point. I picked up a shell before we left and looked at Nicole, "I'm counting on depositing this some day in Alaska!" I winked at her.

The first part of the run was all about learning our rhythm, how we could work together to find the best equilibrium between foot and bike. We entered a forest and climbed a hill, the Paso Garibaldi—three thousand meters (9,843 feet) of unpaved ascent. It was symbolic of the road ahead: uphill, strenuous, but full of reward and beauty. By the time we got to our campsite that night, we were exhausted and sweaty, but utterly full of satisfaction. On that first day we had actually experienced all four seasons: a southern hemisphere summer day as we departed Ushuaia, a cool rain shower and vibrant spring flowers as we ascended the Paso Garibaldi, winter conditions at the top of the pass, and then fall winds as we descended into the headwinds of Patagonia.

It was a wonder to watch Nicole. The girl who grew up in the vineyards was not an outdoorswoman. She had not camped before. She had no idea what it was to sleep and shower and do her business outside. But my girl, she learned quickly.

When she woke up that first morning, she saw a spectacle. To her, it was the Garden of Eden. Everything was peaceful; the fauna was waking up with her; the world was peeling back its eyes and showcasing its beauty that only the early risers are privy to. She took her first shower in a wide-open space, standing naked in the midst of a field, while I heated up the water and got the coffee going.

Nicole peddled her bike towing the small trailer—which we affectionately called "home, sweet home"—for 2,500 miles before the bike was hit by a car and destroyed. Fortunately, she was not injured. We then purchased a motor scooter for her, but the headwinds in Patagonia were so strong that we actually considered flying to Alaska and then running south.

Persistence paid off, and we endured the winds. By then, we were nearly on the doorstep of the Atacama Desert, the driest place on earth outside of Antarctica. At one point in this 1,500-mile desert, we traveled for three days through salt flats never seeing anything alive other than each other.

I loved watching her in that setting, learning the world around her that she had never experienced before. Her eyes were wide as a child's as she learned what all great nature lovers intimately understand: these simple things, these minimal but exquisite pleasures, they are the real values of existence.

CHAPTER TEN

The Last Great Adventure

"The need for change bulldozed a road down the center of my mind."
—Maya Angelou

When I purchased it from the store, it was just a little trinket that would remind me of my work in the mountains. Something Nicole and I could carry with us that wouldn't take up too much space, but something that we could have and look back on years later. Something we could bring from home—a symbol of what was important to us—that could protect us. A talisman of sorts.

The word talisman comes from the Greek word *telein*, which means to initiate into the mysteries. I wouldn't say I'm superstitious or that I give too much credit to the magical, but there are certain tangible things in life that ruffle up your emotions; they bring you back to a place and time where a feeling that you once had becomes very real again.

It was a carabiner. Just a cheap little oblong ring that connects to the eye of a piton to hold a rope, a brand new one that had never been used, and we tossed it in the trailer to come with us on the road and remind us of where we come from in the Alps. And after that little carabiner had traveled up the Pan American Highway, it found its way into the hands of a new owner: my friend, Bertrand Piccard. If I had known the journey it would really take and what it would actually come to mean, perhaps I would have been more careful in choosing the object. But that's just one of life's little bits of humor: you don't always know what will be important to you.

Bertrand and I have never shared a lot of concrete things or moments together, but we do have a lot of respect for one another, which is often so much more valuable than time.

Bertrand was born into a family of firsts. The Piccards were all conquerors of great ideas. Much like a royal family, certain things were passed down from generation to generation. Only it wasn't a crown they inherited, but idealism. Something in the Piccard blood stirred and made them all a bit eager to go and do things that had never been done before. Auguste, Jacques, and Bertrand were the kind of men who made the outlandish palatable.

Auguste Piccard, the grandfather, was born in Basel, Switzerland in 1884. With a mind for physics, Auguste took tea with the illustrious Albert Einstein and the French-Polish physicist Marie Curie. In good company, he carved out his notch in the world by inventing the pressurized cabin and the stratospheric balloon. In 1932, he became the first in humankind to ascend into the stratosphere and observe the curvature of the earth with his own two eyes.

Twenty years later, he flipped his theory on its head. Instead of looking to the heights of the sky, he looked to the depths of the ocean. Keeping the principles of his balloon intact, Auguste built a groundbreaking submarine, which he dubbed the Bathyscaphe. In 1953, partnering with his son, Jacques, they dove in the Bathyscaphe to 3,150 meters. In doing so, he became the man of both extremes. He had flown to the highest and dived to the deepest.

But Auguste Piccard was not all adventure. He was a man of details and intellect, too. A commander of the Legion of Honor and the Order of Leopold, he was a scientist at heart. He assembled the most accurate scales of his era and had a passion for precision which, among his peers, warranted the nickname: "the extra decimal place." Auguste's findings were so crucial, in fact, that an experiment he conducted in a balloon helped prove part of Einstein's Theory of Relativity.

From Auguste, the baton was passed to Jacques, who continued down the diving path. He acquired the World Record for the deepest dive ever—burrowing seven miles down to the bottom of the Marianas Trench.

And then it was on to his son, and my friend, Bertrand. Born in Lausanne, Switzerland, in 1958, Bertrand is one of those guys who has his hands in a little bit of everything. He's a practicing psychiatrist, an aeronaut, and a public speaker.

Studying psychiatry and growing up in the family he did, Bertrand was always interested in seeing how humans behaved in extreme conditions. And like his father and grandfather, he was called to test the limits on himself. In his twenties, still a ripe, strapping boy, he became one of the pioneers of hang gliding. And in 1985, he became the European champion in hang-glider aerobatics.

In 1992, he won the first transatlantic balloon race with Wim Verstraeten. And shortly thereafter, he launched the Breitling Orbiter project with the goal of flying around the world. So many had tried the feat before. And so many had failed, including the billionaire balloonist Richard Branson. His latest attempt had seen the balloon fall into the ocean near Hawaii on Christmas day. But Bertrand would be successful. Along with Brian Jones, a British aeronaut, he completed the first ever non-stop flight around the world in a balloon. They were shocked themselves that it had happened. When the balloon had passed Puerto Rico, their calculations showed that their slow speed would leave them short of fuel; they wouldn't make it to their destination. But then suddenly the speed, for no apparent reason, increased rapidly, over 150 miles per hour.

"Then," Bertrand said, "I just threw all my calculations away." It was a blessing, he said, of a mysterious invisible hand.

Bertrand and Brian's orbit became the longest flight—in distance and duration—in the history of aviation. People called it the last great adventure of the twentieth century.

When Bertrand and Brian stepped off the plane that had brought them from Cairo to Geneva, a trumpeter met them with the "Triumphal March" from "Aida." It was a homecoming fit for a duke. Dignitaries and fans and media clustered around, clapping and hollering.

Even little school children had been given the day off, so they could stand on the tarmac in the slight cold drizzle to see their heroes alight from the plane. Bertrand and Brian, in their dark blue flight suits, were beaming. They gave a victory salute and listened to a short welcoming speech from Swiss Vice President Adolphe Ogi, who quoted Antoine de Saint-Exupery's children's book, "Our little prince came down from the sky and landed in the desert among us."

And landing with them in the desert as well was the carabiner. The very one that had been inside our belongings, running with us for three years along the roads of the American Challenge. In 1999, back in Switzerland, I went to see Bertrand off for the launch of his flight around the world. He had called me three days prior to when he was supposed to take off in his balloon. I was running through Italy at the time, headed back up to Switzerland to see him off, and he was all shakes. "This life is crazy," he said. "I don't feel well. I'm nervous. The weather forecast isn't good. I worry about the wind. Truthfully, I don't know if I have the courage to do this. My two competitors tried and failed, but at least they had the courage to follow through."

Bertrand was like anyone else who has ever had a big dream. He worried that others would see what he wanted to do as stupid, and he didn't want to fail. I, though, knew my friend and knew his courage. The doubts would pass, but the courage would stay. At the starting line I handed him the carabiner that had traveled with me on the American Challenge. "Here's to a little luck," I said.

And he took off. And nineteen days after that, the little prince came down from the sky and landed among us. His courage had won.

A year later, in 2000, Bertrand came to see me off for the World Tour, and he gave me the carabiner that had been so trusty. It brought us luck again, and that one little carabiner that had already traveled the longest road in the world from South America to Alaska, and that had already flown around the world by balloon nonstop, then spent another five years traipsing across six continents. Now the carabiner rests in my home, waiting, I suppose, for the next big adventure.

CHAPTER ELEVEN

The Darien Gap

"The Chinese use two brush strokes to write the word 'crisis.' One brush stroke stands for danger; the other for opportunity. In a crisis, be aware of the danger—but recognize the opportunity."

—John F. Kennedy

After fourteen months on the road, we'd completed South America, but did you know that there is no road between South America and Central America? Only the very dense Darien Jungle, which makes it impossible to build and maintain a road for motor vehicles. There was no way that I was going to take the easy way and cross this segment of the Magic Line by boat or plane. For months, I'd been looking for a way in. Getting in was only half the battle though. The hardest part would be getting through it. But everyone, everywhere, had that same look on their face when I asked them for advice on how to trek through it. A glazed-over roll of the eyes. "You can't possibly be serious," their glances told me. "It's an outlaw area. It's not normal to be there. If you go, you must be an outlaw yourself."

But I was very serious. If I was going to do this trip at all, I was going to do it crossing the Darien Gap.

The Darien Gap is a rather paltry amount of land. Measuring just over ninety-nine miles long and thirty-one miles wide, it's but a speck of dust on the world's shoe. The kind of place that could be brushed off and done with, if only it could be forgotten.

But what you learn on the road, more than anywhere else, is that looks are illusory. It's often not the biggest or most formidable-looking opponent that should cause you to shake like a child. It's the small and unsuspecting things. For example, the Golden Dart Frog. A fluorescent, sunshiny yellow, this little guy—weighing in at only an ounce and stretching to an imposing height of an inch—is native to the rain forests of Colombia. Unfortunately, while you might want to take him home and carry the cute little sucker around in your pocket, you would be sorely misguided to do so. He's cloaked in enough poison to kill your entire extended family without so much as blinking. For years, the tribesmen in Colombia have used the frogs' poison as a weapon, wiping the tips of their darts on the yellow creatures and then shooting the poison-dipped arrows into the camps of their enemies. Hence, the frog's prevailing name, Golden Dart.

Like I said, looks are illusory.

And so it is with the Darien Gap. It's legendary for being one of the last truly unexplored places in the world. Even grand adventurers, full of bravado and daring, hesitate to make their way across these ninety-nine miles. It's become, in its own way, what Mount Everest once was in the mountaineering world—a place where people are told to respect it and steer clear of it if they know what's good for them.

If you pull up a map and find the Gap, you'll see it's just a narrow strip of land, which is flanked by Colombia and Panama. The Colombian side of the Gap is overcome by the delta of the Atrato River, creating a cocktail of marshland and swampland. On the Panama side, it's another face of the coin. The geography is lush—a mountainous rain forest with peaks and valleys from a low of 200 feet to a high of 6,053 feet.

This perplexing strip serves as a filter of sorts between the hardship in South America and the wealth in North America. And it's the one pivotal plot of earth where the Pan-American Highway—a puzzle of roads that crosses the entirety of North, Central, and South America—is disrupted. Treacherous, harmful, and enticing, the Gap is unbroken jungle, teaming with a combination of seduction and severity. It's pristine in portions—unbelievably gorgeous—but all that beauty is flanked by a swarm of ugliness. You can be sure that anything in life that is evil rests its head in the Darien Gap.

Those who live near it know it's chummy with death, a place where few people go in and even fewer go out. Casualties are contagious there, not only as a consequence of the natural forces, which are plenty, but also just as much due to the crippling man-made plagues that have haunted the rainforest for years—namely groups of rebels and offshoot military groups, like the Revolutionary Armed Forces of Colombia (FARC), the National Liberation Army, and the United Self-Defense Forces of Colombia.

These groups are famous for the pastimes of drug dealing, kidnapping, ransom, and killing. And the Darien makes them all the more successful, because in this jungle, there are no watchdogs. No one to sound the alarm if you call out in the night. No one to slap their wrists and take them away when they're caught doing wrong. The only government there is the kind where the sharpest machete wins.

In 2003, while trying to trek the Darien Gap, famed adventurer, Robert Young Pelton, was kidnapped and held for ten days by the United Self Defense Forces of Colombia. "We had probably been traveling a week before it happened," he said. "We set off with three Kuna Indian guides on this route… and at about 11:44 in the morning, three Kuna Indians passed us on the trail, and all of a sudden we heard automatic gunfire for about three minutes, about half a mile [0.8 kilometer] from us. Our guides ran away—they dropped our stuff and just took off. And we had a discussion as a team. I suggested we walk into the ambush as opposed to try to hide or run away. The jungle is very dense, so if [armed men] hear people in the bush, the first thing they do is start shooting. So we decided to talk very loudly in English and keep together as a group and let them know we were coming. It took about half an hour for them to calm down because they were so amped up. I don't know if you know what it's like when you walk into a firefight— but they were wired and twitchy, shouting and yelling. Ultimately they killed four people…."

When asked if he had any advice for would-be Darien travelers, Pelton said, "The Darien Gap is an extremely dangerous place—it's probably the most dangerous place in the Western Hemisphere, definitely in Colombia. It's used as a conduit for drugs. There are no police there, there's no military, the trails aren't marked... unless you have a lot of experience in Colombia, I wouldn't suggest it. The jungle there is not viewed as a place that is pristine and beautiful—it's looked at as a place where you get killed."

For years, countries all over the world have tried to sort out the absent pocket in the Pan-American Highway, insisting that doing a bit of patchwork and building a road through the Gap would be good for so many things—safety, growth. But all efforts have been rather pitiful and fruitless, and so the Gap remains just that—a gap between the safe and the unsafe. Which is why, of course, I had to go.

Nicole and I knew when we started the American Challenge that eventually we'd reach the Gap. She assumed we'd skip over it, letting it be a small blip given the enormity of our trip. But there's nothing more unpleasant to me than a shortcut. I had this magic line shooting straight up to Alaska. My plan had been to run the longest road in the world, and I couldn't let something like a little piece of land force me to break my promise.

So we set out with a new plan. I'd go by boat with Nicole to Panama where I'd drop her off. I'd fly back to Colombia and pass through the Gap on my own. Nicole, though perhaps not as thrilled with the idea as I, agreed, because she understood my commitment to this journey.

And this is where fate came in. On our way over to Panama, I was standing on the deck of the boat and struck up a conversation with a traveler. I was always doing that. Just talking. Just seeing why people were where they were in the world. He was a tough-looking guy, on the heavyset side, and had a pretty impressive motorbike with him. Turns out, he'd been travelling for a while as well. He'd driven over 60,000 miles on his bike and was itching for more.

"You know," he said, "I really wanted to cross the Darien Gap, but there's just no way to do it with the bike. It's impossible. It's too heavy and there's no track. Plus, probably not the best route to go alone."

He laughed at this. As though the idea were mad. As though he were the only one who had ever thought about going.

I had to chuckle at this, too. Really, what are the chances that you'll get two guys on a boat who are just a bit wide-eyed enough to want to pass through drug country? When you're having crazy dreams, you rarely stop to think about how many others might be having them with you. And perhaps if you did, you'd realize your dreams weren't so crazy or impossible after all.

I told Uwe Diemer, a German adventurer, about my Magic Line, and about what Nicole and I had been doing.

"I don't want to break it," I said. "I can't break it."

And he looked at me hard under those big, bushy eyebrows and said what had become a very common phrase to my ears, "Are you crazy?"

"Are you with me?" I said, a slight twinkle in my eye.

And he smiled, "Of course. Yes."

We made a deal to meet back up on the Colombian side in two days' time, and we'd cross the gap together. I'd map out a route and get supplies, and we'd source out a boat when we met up. I was sure I could have crossed it alone, but if I'm being honest, I was relieved. There's safety in numbers, even if it's only false safety.

On our two-day break, I went searching for a map. I headed down to a remote GI military camp in Panama that was swathed in dust and humidity. I knew it was the only place where I could get a good land map of the area. The Darien isn't exactly the type of locale where you can go get a nice charted print out at your local convenience store.

I didn't have much luck there though. The general, a broad, though even-keeled man, looked at me sorely.

"Do you know what you're trying to do?" he said. "This isn't a good place to be going. I can't recommend it."

I laughed. "Not many people have."

He scratched his freshly-shaven face and waited for me to sober up. But I insisted.

"Whether you recommend it or not, I'm going. And if I could have a map, you'd make our chance of success that much better."

He wasn't terribly moved.

"Take a look," he said. "Write down some notes. But you can't take it with you."

And so that's what I did.

Two days later, with my chicken-scratch directions in hand, I met up with my friend as planned, and we started our journey through the Darien Gap. The first step is crossing the river. The Atratro River is huge. It's far too wide to swim; you have to hire a boat. But getting a guide, that's a trick in itself. We asked at least ten people, but no one was interested. They shook their heads smiling. They knew if they left us at the entrance of the Gap, they would probably never see us again. And that was one of the most curious things about the Darien. For a place that is so hardened and cruel and relentless, no one wanted to be responsible for taking us to our death. They couldn't stomach the thought of it.

Finally, though, we found a less concerned soul.

"Why do you want to go there?" he said.

I looked him squarely in the face, trying hard not to laugh. I was tired of the same story and the same rejections, so I tried something new.

"I'm very interested in conducting a study on butterflies. I've heard there are some fascinating ones in the Darien Gap that can be seen nowhere else!"

He cocked his eyes at me and smiled a knowing smile. Apparently he'd found a man of a kindred spirit—another man who didn't tell the truth.

"Meet me at five in the morning. We'll head over straightaway."

It was dark when we left. We climbed into a flat, metal boat in a little fishing harbor. There was stillness all around us. We went slowly out of the harbor for two or three minutes, but when he hit the open water, we went flying. He kicked up his two engines and jumped over the waves as though we were a mere pebble being skipped across water. I was pretty certain the boat would tip over, that we'd meet our end before we even got to the Darien Gap.

"Slow down," I called to him. "We're in no hurry. Ten minutes or a half-hour journey, I don't care."

But he just looked back at me and smiled, a knowing wink hidden there somewhere in his face, "The local police only have one engine. This one goes twice as fast."

And that's when I knew that our "chauffeur" was a drug dealer.

We made it across, alive, and began what would be a twelve-day trek across the gap. It was a tough hike. You're wet twenty-four hours a day, hiking for no less than thirteen hours, just showering in your sweat. You spend your nights in a hammock, and the next morning you can barely discern where you had macheteed your way in the previous day. Every day you eat the same servings of rice and soup. The number of mosquitoes, monkeys, and snakes that you encounter is incomprehensible. You hear noises and you flinch, unsure if what you heard was the call of an animal or the cracking of a twig or the steps of a man with a machete who's just waiting for you to make the next move. And you pray to God with as much sincerity as you ever have that you just don't come across anyone. That those sounds are just sounds, not people. Because if you do, you're pretty certain that you won't get out of this place alive.

The trek for me was hard. But I'd been conditioning for it, running those twenty to thirty miles a day. But for Uwe, it was more taxing. He'd been riding on his bike. The endurance he'd built up was quite different. But he pulled up something from down deep in his soul and made it all the way through.

When we finally got out of the impossible Darien Gap, Uwe and I parted ways, and I went to find Nicole in Panama. Before leaving, I had told her to expect me to be gone twenty days. If it was more than that, she could be pretty certain I was lost forever. Send out the search party, sure, but don't be surprised when they find nothing.

Through the generosity of a guy from the UBS bank, she'd been set up in a five-star hotel while I was sloshing through the rainforest. And while she'd been basking in the sun in comfort, she was totally uncomfortable with this uneasy feeling of doubt. Every day on the local news she heard about the myriad of awful things happening in the Darien Gap. How many bodies they'd found. How many people had gone missing. She'd go to bed at night trembling with the knowledge that she might never see me again.

When I finally arrived in the city, it was close to three in the morning. I hadn't had a shower in two weeks. I was waterlogged and sweaty, caked in a heavy dust and mud. I didn't have a key to Nicole's room, so I went to the front desk.

"Excuse me, ma'am," I said. "I need a key to Nicole Roetheli's room."

She looked at me curiously, studying my appearance.

"I'm sorry, sir. I'm not permitted to do that. How do you know this person?"

"I'm her husband," I said.

And again she looked at me, not really believing one of the clients of their five-star hotel would be traipsing in at three in the morning, looking like a homeless man from the gutter.

"Listen," I said. "Can you call her? She can verify who I am and then you can send me up. Will that work?"

The woman hesitated, but finally obliged. She called up to Nicole's room, confirmed who I was, and then passed the phone along to me.

"Nicole!" I said. "In thirty seconds I will be in your bed!" Then I hung up the phone and jumped the staircase, forgetting there might be protocol in establishments like these. But, when you get home and return to the one person you absolutely adore, you don't worry about protocol. You're not concerned about making a scene. You just want to be in her arms as soon as possible.

I got to the room, took a quick, much-needed shower, and climbed into Nicole's arms and the clean, 600 thread-count sheets.

"You won't believe it," I told her climbing into bed. "We saw the most magnificent butterflies!"

CHAPTER TWELVE

The Necessities

"One must maintain a little bittle of summer, even in the middle of winter."

—Henry David Thoreau

Fire. There were few things we had to have to live on the road, but fire was one of them. It's a life giver; it warms everything around it. You need it to make your coffee and cook your meals. But it's also your presence, your friends and your family. They are across oceans, sleeping at different times of the day, but somehow when the spark hits and the smoke drafts into the air, a warmness settles that was absent just moments prior.

Right now, it's dark outside, and if I lit a candle, everyone would draw near, because that's the light, and people are drawn to the light. The same is true with fire around the world. And that was very important on the tour. With camping, all the time you're alone outside, in these solitary places, miles and miles from any sort of humanity, but when we would build a wood fire, a sense of comfort would envelop us.

Out of the 1,910 nights of the World Tour, on over 1,200 of those we built a fire. Most of the time it just took a few minutes of poking around where we'd set our tent down to find a good piece of wood or two, but other times it took longer. We weren't always in the most convenient places.

In the Atacama Desert, there was practically no hope of finding wood anywhere, so we'd have to improvise. We knew we had to have fire on those nights, because the desert temperatures could drop and be remarkably cold despite the heat of the day. So we'd keep our eyes peeled. When you're going seven miles an hour, you have the luxury of being able to see everywhere. You can look in the nooks and crannies. Sometimes trucks would drive through the empty deserts and, for no good reason at all, would lose a piece of wood here or there. Or perhaps a piece of debris. Whenever Nicole or I spotted something, she'd pull over, pick up the piece of wood, and throw it in the trailer. At the end of the day, you'd be surprised how much we had found. Surviving on the road is about improvisation, if nothing else.

When we'd get to the campsite at night, I'd take out the machete, cut up the pieces of wood, and build a fire under a thousand million stars in the middle of nowhere. Those peaceful nights by the warmth of dancing flames were some of the loveliest I've ever had.

When people ask about stories from the road, they want to hear about the limits. They want to hear about encounters with cheetahs, being surrounded by men at gunpoint, and the depths of Nicole's sickness. And I can understand that. We all want to be compelled.

But, no matter what adventure you take, your pulse is not going to be racing 100 percent of the time. There is a basic amount of living and simplicity that gets you from day to day. You have to have things like fire, and you have to plan your logistics well.

We didn't carry much with us on the tour, but anything we had was with us all the time, because not a bit of it was unnecessary. We tried to be very efficient, so we were conscious not to waste our space or energy on things that just took up room but added no value.

With me all the time was Nicole. She was not a material item, of course, but having Nicole with me was as crucial as having a set of matches or a drop of water.

We also always had the bike, the trailer, some spare parts to fix those two pieces of equipment, one tent, two sleeping bags, one pot for coffee, one pot for spaghetti, two plastic bowls, two spoons, the machete, one video camera, one picture camera, one spare pair of running shoes, a bag of clothes—one for Nicole and one for me, a tarp to cover the trailer, a small pharmacy bag for medical emergencies, a bag of food, a minimum of six two-liter bottles of coke, a jerry can with water, and a jerry can with gasoline.

We also carried with us a press book detailing what we were doing and some pictures from home. Sometimes these served as our passports, giving us the ability to share our story when it otherwise might have been hard to explain. We wanted people to understand who we were and where we were coming from. And the responses from people were always emotional and vivid. Can you imagine showing a guy on the Atacama Desert, who has never seen precipitation fall from the sky, a picture of Switzerland with waterfalls and mountains and snow and trees?

Yes, sometimes even the simple things can make you lose your breath.

CHAPTER THIRTEEN

A New Vision

"There is no exercise better for the heart than reaching down and lifting people up."

—John Holmes

When we finished the American Challenge in Fairbanks on December 4, 1997, it was brutally cold. Alaskan cold, which isn't a kind of cold you feel anywhere else in the world. It had been under the freezing point for two months. We were camping outside, constantly aware of the elements. No one was on the road. If you think about utter desolation, that's basically what we had endured.

Our welcome home was not, to say the least, slated for the best time of the year. There are pockets of months when Alaska has a summer warmth and kindness that you want to flock to. You want to fish and hunt and take part in everything it means to be living in the depths of nature. But the winter, it's a beast. Then it's sometimes hard for people to just get out of the house. And yet, people came to welcome us. Perhaps not as many as we had hoped for, but Guy Fournier, a licensed gold prospector and a pursuer of dreams, had met us two weeks before in the midst of the Alaskan desolation, waving a flag of Valais, and had organized an event with a bunch of friends and some journalists.

People from the town had come across the slippery roads or on their bikes and were standing out there, huddled together in the cold, waiting for us to turn the bend.

When we took that final step of the 24,115-kilometer [14,984-mile] journey, there were shouts of jubilation, relief, and a hurry to get back somewhere warm.

I was talking and shaking hands, a bit shocked by the whole thing really, and there was this one guy in the mix, whom I didn't know at the time, who came over and shook my hand. Later, I would find out his name was Ron Zamber. He looked at me, and I'll never forget what he said, "What you did is a great inspirational story for me. I'm an eye surgeon here; I manage a clinic, and what you did with your running trip really gives me some ideas of what I can do to help some kids, too. Anyway, congratulations. And welcome home."

That was that and he left, and I didn't hear from Ron for a couple of years.

Now, let's flash forward to the World Tour. Nicole and I were in the middle of nowhere, about halfway through our journey, when we got some bad news. The worst news, really. The Swiss charity that had been running our Fan Club and supporting our efforts to make the world aware of the plight of children through the World Tour Run for Kids was backing out. I hadn't been so disappointed in anything since the Olympics in 1976 when I wasn't able to box. This, though, seemed even more brutal. When you've got so many miles on your legs and so much invested, it's a death toll to hear your main supporter has lost faith. They said they had lots of reasons. To me, none of them sounded like good ones. The charity was just another "Doubting Thomas".

With that support gone, it was a huge blow. Not only because they were helping to funnel in donors, but more so, because running for kids had given us a great purpose. There was a reason to run thirty more miles tomorrow. And the next day. And the next. The Run for Kids wasn't just about proving something to ourselves. It was about really helping people. We could continue on without them. Sure, of course. But at the end of the day, the reason you do something is just as important as actually doing it.

I wracked my brain constantly for ways to refresh our humanitarian connection with the tour and, out of nowhere, I remembered the man on the finish line in Fairbanks. I couldn't remember his name, only that he was an eye doctor who wanted to find his own way to help. I figured Fairbanks wasn't such a big place; surely he'd be easy to find. And shockingly, he was. Sitting there in an Internet shop in Malaysia, I looked up his number and gave him a call.

He was exactly the same way on the phone as my mental image from the finish line. He was full of energy, bright and kind. He told me he'd changed his life since the last time I had seen him. He'd travelled overseas multiple times to perform eye surgeries in third world countries, giving people back their sight in places such as Ecuador, Malawi, and Nepal. For as little as 150 Swiss Francs, he could heal a person with cataracts. He told me about this one man in Nepal, an elderly gentleman with wrinkles set into his face like ironed folds. He'd never seen anything in his life. He had no idea what the world looked like. What shape the grass was; what color the lilies were. It had always just been a dark canvas. His wife came with him to the surgery, only allowing herself the smallest bit of hope, but the procedure went well. When he finally opened his eyes, he could see his wife. "My wife, you are even more beautiful than before." As you can imagine, everyone was crying.

I was thrilled to hear of his humanitarian efforts. You remember a man vaguely and it turns out he's exactly whom you've been looking for and exactly who you were hoping he would be. If there were a man who understood what it meant to help people, Ron was the one. I told him our situation, what had happened, and what we were looking for.

He laughed and said straightaway that he thought I was crazy to run more than the 15,000 miles we'd already covered in the American Challenge, but that he wanted to stay in touch. Maybe we could make something work.

I could hear the wheels turning in his head and let him muse it over. We conversed off and on, and eventually he decided that while he would love to come visit us, it wasn't possible because of his busy eye surgery schedule in Alaska.

"How about this?" he said. "I'd love to help you. Why don't I pay for your flights and you can come here to Fairbanks. We'll work out all the details here in nature's beauty."

I remembered an immense feeling of possibility stepping off that plane. As though for every door in the world that had just been bolted shut, a new one was flung open.

I don't think Nicole or I ever would have imagined a day when we would return to Fairbanks, the final point of our Magic Line in the American Challenge. We had been there; it had served its significant purpose. There was more to see and do. And there were certainly places that were warmer!

It had been six years, but the place was always etched into our minds as important, and now it would become vitally more so on the World Tour.

Nicole and I flew from Australia, where we were at the time, to Fairbanks where we met Ron, his wife Susan, and their kids. Alaska was exactly the way we had left it—save for the freezing temperatures—and the people there remembered us. In two to three days' time, we hammered out the details and just like that, Ron Zamber blew fresh hope into our run. We signed on the dotted line and then flew to Auckland, New Zealand, refreshed and ready to continue the Run for Kids.

"This is what you're running for," he said. "You should see it."

I was talking to Ron on the phone. We were in South America, about to hit Rio. Ron and I kept in touch pretty frequently. He was invested in us now, and we were certainly invested in him and what he was doing. By then Nicole and I had run the South Pacific and had made our way through most of South America. In just a few weeks, that continent would come to a close, too, when we hit Rio de Janeiro and the 21,462nd mile on our journey. Ron suggested that once we hit Rio, we should come back up to Fairbanks for a quick charity run and then go with him to Costa Rica on one of his missions.

Nicole and I agreed. This was definitely worth a pause in our journey.

It was June of 2004, and after a week in Rio trying to obtain our U.S. visa, we headed up once more to Fairbanks. The Zambers were having a run to benefit International Vision Quest, their nonprofit. All the money raised would go toward helping Ron's surgical missions abroad. For once, I didn't have to run by myself! A 5k-run in 86-degree weather with 120 others. It was like Christmas. We raised about 3,600 Swiss Francs. It was a modest amount, but it would pay for the operations of at least thirty patients with cataracts. It could even buy a few hundred people glasses.

When the run was over, we had about a week's time before we were scheduled to leave for Costa Rica. Ron invited me, as promised, to his clinic. He let me be as involved as he could, which was a thrill. I washed my hands, put on the mask and watched a master eye surgeon perform his magic. Cataract surgery, as you can imagine, is pretty intricate. The cloudy lens is removed from the eye and replaced with an artificial lens. Most patients see clearly the next day. Watching Ron stand over his patients, I held my breath. Vision was a game of accuracy. If he moved one millimeter, the person on the table could be blind. So he'd stand there over the patient and operate for a full minute, not breathing. Then he'd take a step back, take a long deep breath, and then go at it again. It was nothing short of a miracle.

The wildfire erupted near Fairbanks on Friday, four days before our flight was set to leave. At first it was on the fringes, far away. Just taunting us, like a small child. But soon enough it surrounded the city, buckling it down on all sides. The forest was twenty to thirty miles away, but as you can imagine, with wind, twenty to thirty miles is nothing in Alaska.

As the days progressed, the fire got worse. A dense smoke filled the sky. The air became unbreathable. A stench filled the air, so pungent you could taste it. We watched from the windows as it came closer and closer, and inevitably we got the call that we would have to evacuate. Everyone in the area between the Chena River and the road linking Fairbanks to Circle would have to go. Everyone was encouraged to wear a filter mask and stay inside safe houses. Don't panic, the officials said. But it was hard. There were nearly sixty forest fires burning in Alaska, several of which were spread out over hundreds of acres. And the lightening, which continued to pierce the sky, didn't help.

Ron's house was in a particularly risky area. And twenty-four hours before we left, we set to evacuating the house. We carried out the essentials, beginning with his two children, the two dogs and cats, and a few precious belongings. We headed toward the home of one of his friends who lived in a safe zone. It had been more than twenty years since Alaska had experienced a situation of this magnitude. We spent the night listening to the news. It was a city undergoing shock.

I took Ron aside that night. We could see the orange glow of the fire in the distance.

"You know," I told him, "We don't have to go tomorrow. Your house is on the fringe. It could burn. I understand if you need to be here." And I meant it. Even though I didn't have a home, I could understand the value of one. I could understand the pain that would happen if he lost it.

But Ron shrugged it off.

"No, of course we'll go. It's much more important to save some kids than to save a house."

The week in Costa Rica was such a pure, cleansing reminder. It was intense, to be sure, and brimming with emotion, but Nicole and I were reinvigorated with purpose. Ron and his assistants did checkups for 592 people, of which eighty-seven were orphaned children. In the most affluent countries, blessed with the best health and material wealth, I'd never seen such hope, joy, and pure thankfulness as I did in this place of scarcity. I filmed every day, capturing the moving stories through the lens, while Nicole welcomed patients and administered eye drops, so their pupils could be dilated. Everyone worked around the clock, from early in the morning until far after the sun had gone down. There was simply so much to do, so much need in the world.

"Are you not tired?" I asked my friend Ron one evening.

"There is time to be tired later," he said. "Now is the time to do good."

CHAPTER FOURTEEN

The Circumference of the World

"As long as my heart's still in it, I'll keep going. If the passion's there, why stop?.... There'll likely be a point of diminishing returns, a point where my strength will begin to wane. Until then, I'll just keep plodding onward, putting one foot in front of the other to the best of my ability. Smiling the entire time."

—Dean Karnazes

It started at the finish line, which is, admittedly, a very peculiar place to start something. But as soon as we arrived in Fairbanks, Alaska, at the end of the American Challenge, I knew I wasn't done. I knew I could keep running. Before we left, I wasn't proud enough to say I would succeed. No, that would have been childish. I only promised I wouldn't quit. There's a big difference there. I told everyone I was ready to go far, very far, and why not until the end? And here it was, three years in the making, and we had made it to the finish line. And while I was excited for a warm bed and some decent rest, more than either of those things I wanted to keep going.

While the band was playing at full force and the small crowd was huddled together, bending into one another for warmth, I leaned over to Nicole and whispered in her ear, "How about starting all over again?"

And Nicole, my bride, she didn't hesitate. In the same way she had pointed to the bottom of Argentina, to Tierra del Fuego, she answered me. Her eyes were courageous and excited. She didn't have to say anything. Her answer was understood: Yes! Of course.

And that's precisely how the World Tour emerged, at the very end of a 15,000-mile journey. It was December of 1997 then, and we wouldn't set out on to the World Tour until February of 2000, giving us roughly two years to work out all the logistics.

And the logistics wouldn't be easy. I imagined they might go a little more smoothly than they had the first time. People would see that Nicole and I had done this before—we could do it again! But there are so many people who don't want to believe in dreams. They want to believe in cold hard facts. And cash. And a sundry of other details that take all the magic out of it. And yet those details are necessary, just as the logistics are necessary.

The idea came to us pretty simply. We knew whatever we did next would have to be bigger and better. We would have to push ourselves to accomplish a new feat. And since we'd already run the longest highway in the world, biting off 15,000 miles, whatever was next would have to be impressively large. And how much larger can you really get than the world?

People are often confused by the phrase "run the world." They look at the pliable lines of continents bending into water, they look at the mass of space, and they scratch their heads not entirely sure how to do the math. But in truth it's rather simple. To run the world is to run the distance of the circumference of the earth at its widest point—the equator—a remarkable 40,075.16 kilometers (24,901.055 miles).

Our initial goal was to run through Switzerland and France, followed by Morocco, Mauritania, Senegal, Guinea, the Ivory Coast, Ghana, Togo, Benin, Nigeria, Cameroon, Congo, Zaire, Uganda, Rwanda, Burundi, Tanzania, Madagascar, Egypt, Gaza, Jordan, Lebanon, Syria, Iraq, Kuwait, Sri Lanka, India, Nepal, Bangladesh, Thailand, Vietnam, Singapore, Australia, Brazil, Chile, Peru, Ecuador, Colombia, Haiti, the United States, and then back to Switzerland through Spain and France.

This, of course, wouldn't be the end route. So much happens between when you leave home and when you return to it. In our case, civil wars broke out and 9/11 occurred. There were some countries we simply couldn't get into. Or, even if we could, we would have been shot straight upon arrival.

The first major changing point was in Africa as we were headed into Guinea. There was constant instability along the border. Countless villages had been burned and pillaged. People had been massacred with machetes and women had been raped by rebels from Sierra Leone and Liberia. One night we were staying in a neighborhood where the vast majority of huts were burned to the ground. Children and adults were screaming in the streets, and 407 individuals were macheteed to death in a tribal attack.

The forest area that we would have had to pass through (Macenta) had sustained heavy human losses. The roads were closed and guarded by soldiers, and there was no possible way to enter the Ivory Coast. Guinea, though a democratic country that had never known war, was in a state of alert. We weren't at a greater risk because of our skin; the roots of the conflict were inter-ethnic. But just the same, as Nicole said, "It's best not to tempt the devil." So instead, we departed for the opposite side of the country, then branched off into Mali, Burkina Faso, and Togo. That change cost us the "trifling sum" of 800 additional kilometers (497 miles), which is equal to about a month of running. We added on the countries of South Africa, Swaziland, and Mozambique. It was in Togo where I was stricken with my severe case of malaria—a different variety than Nicole contracted later. For three hours, Nicole was desperately searching—running all over town—to locate a competent doctor to treat my 106-degree (F) temperature in a land where she knew no one! The problem was compounded by the fact that it was a holiday and everyone was enjoying the festivities. The doctor she finally located and who treated me told Nicole that had she not found a competent doctor for another three to five hours, I would have been dead. But with his help I recovered, and the World Tour continued.

In the end, we also cut out Iraq and Iran, due to the events of 9/11, as well as a portion of South America—Peru, Ecuador, Colombia, and Haiti—and in its place put Argentina and Brazil.

After the puzzle had been pieced together though, the resulting sum still remained well above our mark. When we made it back to Switzerland in 2005, we had lapped the earth.

CHAPTER FIFTEEN

Human Warmth

"We cannot live only for ourselves. A thousand fibers connect us with our fellow men; and among those fibers, as sympathetic threads, our actions run as causes, and they come back to us as effects."

—Herman Melville

The human element cannot be underestimated. The love. The effort. The warmth. The magnified potential you have when someone can just reach out and touch you. A million times on the road we fluctuated between solitude and congestion, company and isolation, and we always found an encouraging word—or even a mere look—from another human being provided a fuel to my heart and feet that could not be found elsewhere.

We were on the outskirts of Eassouira. Every pocket of earth on the Moroccan coastline reminded us of Patagonia, the lost and forgotten land. Out there you focus first on the magnitude. The completely bottomless stretches of land that arch into the sky, separating you from the horizon. The distance between towns is immense, and the gaps of time are patched together by long arches of thirsty desert and craggy coastlines. It is not one landscape, but many. Families of panoramas knit into one another, forming a panoramic image fit for Ansel Adams.

You know where you are, you are certain of it, but some part of the surroundings makes you have an out-of-body experience, as though you're traveling with one leg in one part of the world, and one in the other. One minute it seems like the Outback while the next it feels remarkably like a Scottish coastline, the deep blue waters foaming at their tips. There can be few places in the world where the domestic clashes with the otherworldly in such a distinct, tranquil mix. The dogs, the cats, and the horses share land with the armadillos and ostriches. The endangered Mediterranean monk seal shares the coastline with the marbled duck and the Algerian hedgehog. The desert houses the Dorcas gazelle and the golden jackal.

I had been running for five hours. At times that felt long, at times that felt short, and sometimes, like that day, it just felt like each minute was draining me. I could feel my thirst creeping up my throat, my hunger waking up lethargically from a long nap. In moments like that, when the running got the best of me, I looked around and everything that was going on in the periphery seemed so effortless. A slight wind rustled up the sand. The motorcycle hummed. Nicole, with poise, drove on like the miles hadn't fazed her in the least. But my legs were cement. Heavy, tired strides. No, you could hardly call them that. My lips were dry, splintered from the warm sun. My tongue felt heavy in my mouth, like it was taking up too much space. Salt from sweat caked my brow and trickled down my arms and legs, clammy evidence of the difficult stride. I was exhausted.

Nicole forced me to stop and eat something. She could always tell when my resolution was waning. We settled onto the side of the path as I chugged down Coca Cola and shoved down three granola bars. After thirty minutes, we trudged on.

At the next cusp of a town we approached, an old beggar woman was hunched down in the streets, the hem of her dress soaked in week-old sand. She came near us. Her face was beaten down, wrinkled and folded. She extended a shaking hand in our direction, and Nicole handed her three dirhams. Grateful, the woman took Nicole's hand and delicately placed it on her cheek. And a kind, animated smile enveloped her lips. It was enchanting. And that split second reminded us why we were running.

There are moments when you feel ill-equipped. When everyone else's doubt will come down in heavy rains, prying open a slit inside your mind that maybe, just maybe, you weren't cut out for this kind of adventure. And then, someone reaches out and touches you, and just like that you're recharged. The heaviness that seemed so overbearing is now but a splinter. Yes, it is still there, but it is nothing to trifle over. Nothing to keep you from taking the next step.

That night, we pitched our tent, refreshed, on a bluff that had panoramic views all around. The sea splashed up against the rock creating a fan of sprinkles. We each got three liters of water for a shower—a luxury after five days of nowhere to get clean. I danced on the bluffs naked, singing and leaping. Nicole was a bit more shy, hiding behind the larger rocks as she let the pitchers dump down upon her.

We sat down to kindle a fire and, within moments, the police arrived. They questioned us thoroughly and told us we had to leave immediately. Apparently just a few months prior, some other tourists were attacked in that same spot and were savagely raped and beaten. The police escorted us to the station, and we slept there for the night. What luck!

In the morning, we left Agadir and were at the gateway of the Sahara. One thousand seven hundred and twenty kilometers (1,069 miles) down, and infinite vast sands before us.

CHAPTER SIXTEEN

Camels and Big Beauty

"The greatest wealth is to live content with little."

—Plato

We entered the Sahara Desert at its peak. It was June by then, the hottest time of the year. We hadn't planned on being in Mauritania then, but since our departure from Switzerland was forty-five days late, well, luck would have us in the thick of the Sahara in summer.

Mauritania is a small country, but compared to Switzerland, it's huge. And yet, there are only two to three million people there. That's nothing at all really, especially when you consider that ninety-eight percent of the country is pure desert. And while the traveling nomads that haunt the sand dunes are wealthy and stocked full of provisions, the people in the towns are in the deepest pocket of poverty. During the American Challenge, we had already brushed up against poverty quite often, yet Mauritania surpassed even that. We had been warned: in Africa, to be poor is to be truly poor, to possess nothing. But what is most amazing is that the people with the least were the ones to never complain. They were blessed with a constant, small smile.

Nicole and I spent a month there—no more—but every moment was vivid, long, and memorable.

In Mauritania, wealth is not measured in dollars—not in property or attire or vehicles. It's measured in camels. A human's relationship with his camels is not something that we Westerners can understand. Camels are their source of provision, and for centuries have provided many gifts, both in terms of human fuel and transport. Primarily, camels can provide an immense amount of milk. Right after giving birth, female camels can generate more than a gallon of milk per day for somewhere between nine to eighteen months. And for the Saharan nomads, this milk, occasionally mixed with a little camel blood, is their solitary source of sustenance. The milk can be used not only to drink, but also turned into butter and cheese and, once fermented, into alcohol.

On top of this, the camels are also the means of transportation, taking you from one parched spot of land to the next. Regardless of the weather—the scorching heat or the deadening cold—most camels can take you twenty-five to thirty miles a day while hauling over three hundred pounds on their backs. Some breeds can do more than that. The camels are such a vital aspect of desert culture that I was shocked to often see men treating their camels better than their wives.

Nicole and I knew that the only way we would make it across the desert was if we accepted hospitality from the nomads. The Sahara is a fluid place. Camps go up one day, complete with tents and families and nourishment, and the next they vanish as though they had never been there. They have no fixed base. They move about constantly.

But the nomads are smart and intentional, not chaotic. They know how important it is to have shelter from the sun's rays. From ten or eleven o'clock in the morning to six or seven at night, you're forced to take shelter under a tent. It's just too oppressive to be outside.

So you take their hospitality. And the best way they have to say, "Welcome,"—just like we would share a cup of tea or a glass of water—is to offer you a huge bowl of camel's milk, almost half a gallon. And while the thick mixture already doesn't taste very good, you have to remember that it's very hot outside and there's no way to keep the milk cool, so it curdles. And the wind is blowing the whole time, so there are little bits of grass and sand in the milk, floating around like ice cubes. And you have to drink it no matter what. If you don't drink the welcome milk, it means you don't accept their hospitality.

The first day in the Sahara, Nicole choked down a small portion of her welcome drink. In minutes, she was hunched over, hurling it all up. I could get it down, and did, but it was the worst drink I've ever had in my life. And every day, for a month, while we were in Mauritania, I had to drink it.

The fascinating thing about that drink, too, is that it's the drink they give in excess to their teenage girls, those in the puberty range between twelve to fourteen years of age. Each year, they round up all the teenage girls and take them out to a remote area. They feed the girls camel's milk for four to six months to get them as fat as possible. There, the fatter you are, the richer you will be. And while the girl is away gaining weight, her parents are at home finding a husband for her. When she comes back, she's as fat as possible and ready to be married.

And that's one of the reasons why they looked down on me so much. I remember when we crossed over into Mauritania. At the border control, I went through first. And the officer there looked back at Nicole and said, "Is that your wife?" He sounded disappointed already.

"Yes," I said.

"You should throw her away," he said, sifting through my passport.

I looked at him, amazed.

"And why is that?" I asked.

"She is too skinny," he said, scoffing. "No one will want her."

To them, the fact that I had a skinny wife meant that I wasn't rich or powerful. It was the same, too, when they saw that I was the one running and she was the one riding.

"It shouldn't be that way," one man said to me. "You should be the one riding and she should be forced to run."

Yet, no less than twenty times while we were there, someone asked me, "And how many camels would it take to buy your wife?"

Their logic blew my mind. The people are living out there in their nomad shelter in the middle of nowhere, and the men arrive at night in luxury four-wheel drive cars with satellite phones, GPS, and technology from the twenty-first century, but they are living with five-hundred-year-old customs.

❖ ❖ ❖ ❖

We passed the three thousand kilometer mark (1,864 miles) in the Sahara Desert. The place branded us with a red-hot iron. Even though we ran early in the morning, getting up as early as two a.m. to skip the sun's rays, we couldn't escape the heat. Stride after stride, the temperature rapidly increased, the desert drying up right before our eyes. It wouldn't take long for the thermometer to reach 118 degrees. And even though we drank up to twenty liters of liquids a day, I still suffered greatly from severe dehydration, so much so that I even had blood in my urine.

There was a harshness to the place, too, that just grated on our morale. The poverty, the customs, the barrenness of the land. The only true comfort in the Sahara was the kindness of its peculiar people and the nighttime, when you're surrounded by dunes and lifted up into blackness. And there, above your head, are galaxies you couldn't see in any city, spotlights looking down on you with their bright, glowing lights.

When we left Mauritania, we had the feeling we were leaving a country from another time, from another world, from another generation. We were moving about constantly in a universe that was not ours.

Just as we were leaving the capital city, Nicole caught sight of a little boy crouching underneath a table to avoid the heat. She walked to him slowly and handed him a bottle of water. His body reeked, and his eyes were reddened by the sand. He squinted them, as if to thank her. Nicole asked his name and his age, but the question that worried her the most was how long it had been since he had bathed.

"Well over two months," he said.

It was painful for us to sit there and leave him be. How we would have loved to take him to a shower and pile on some fresh, clean clothes.

But what you learn in a place like Mauritania, more than anywhere else, is that you can't force your customs and your expectations on people from a different world.

Parts of the world are as they are because they want to be that way.

Sometimes, no matter how contrary it is to your heart, you just have to leave things be.

CHAPTER SEVENTEEN

Alms

"He who is kind to the poor lends to the LORD, and he will reward him for what he has done."

—Proverbs 19:17

We were in Senegal when Nicole met them, at the village of Kedougou, just on the border of Guinea. You're in the midst of Africa there, seemingly cut off from everything.

We walked to the post office that morning, which is a funny thing to even say, given the situation. We followed the sign that read "Main post office this way," winding down the dirt road until we came to the end of the road where there was a wooden table and two chairs. Apparently, that was their grand postal point!

Nicole and I were, admittedly, a little on edge. For the past three days I'd been trying to rest, getting over a bout of tendonitis that had been flaring up. And in a day's time, we'd be embarking into jungle territory, where roads were mere muddy and capricious trails where no one would come to your rescue.

A voice off to the side asked for alms, but Nicole and I both pretended not to hear. Sometimes, encounters with strangers can leave you shaken, and since we were already in a fragile state, why bother shaking it up even more?

I went off to make a phone call back home and left Nicole standing by the table.

The voice asked a second time, "Madam, alms."

Nicole, on edge perhaps, yelled back at him: "You're out of luck. As for me, I only give something when someone doesn't ask for anything."

Instead of being mad, the three men broke out in laughter, understanding that the woman was in a bad mood. Their voices sounded joyful.

Nicole, blessed with not only a short temper but also a good conscience, immediately felt bad. She turned around and found three old men in broad-brimmed hats. Hats so big you could barely catch a glimpse of their faces. These men, though old, were not ordinary. They no longer had feet, hands, or faces. They were mere stumps full of monstrous deformities. The work of leprosy.

The guilt compounded tenfold, and Nicole reached into her pocket and took out three coins, one for each. And as she gave them each their coin, she leaned over to hug and kiss them.

CHAPTER EIGHTEEN

Susceptible to the Unknown

"Human beings are made up of flesh and blood, and a miracle fiber called courage."

—General George Patton

We stood in the warehouse in Mozambique. People were running around in all directions. It was chaos, both of bodies and words. Cardboard cluttered the floors. Boxes were stacked ground to ceiling. Men in badly faded blue uniforms lifted and hauled and assembled.

There are some places in the world where it still feels like nothing is new. Everything is used over and over again. Worn down to the salt of its beginnings. And so it was in Mozambique, as we stood in the hulk of the shipyard, waiting for the motorcycle to load. In the shipping process, you stand, you watch, you answer, and you pack, but, most importantly, you pray that somehow everything makes it to the destination. This, in some way, is always the practice. A lot of hope mixed with chaos and patience.

Shipping our motorcycle was tedious, but necessary. And getting it from one destination to another was a drain on our time and mind. It tried my patience. You forget, sometimes, when you live in a first world country that acts that should seem so simple, so efficient, can become,

The 25,000 Mile Love Story

in other places, these chaotic underground happenings. People raising their voices. Bribes exchanged under—and over—the table. Duct tape fastening together boxes that look no sturdier than a hurricane-ravaged dock.

The process of shipping the motorcycle from Mozambique to Madagascar is the same old story until two hearses pull into the warehouse. All of a sudden, just like that, the bustle stops. The men stop hauling, running, talking. In their faded uniforms and their unshaven faces, they bow their heads in silence and respect. Two wooden caskets are pulled from the belly of the hearse and two people—young or old, male or female, who knows?—are moved from the cars to crates. They are being returned home. Next door I can hear the workers laughing, carrying on with the joy of life. The contrast is remarkable. How quickly life is taken away. And how quickly the world remembers to turn.

The day had been a good one. By then, we'd been on the road for eighteen months. My feet had pounded the earth for nearly 6,500 miles at a steady, reliable pace of 7.4 miles per hour. I'd worn through eighteen pairs of shoes while traversing fourteen countries, and we'd recently crossed over from Mozambique to Madagascar.

I'd been looking forward to this leg of our route. Madagascar is like no other place you'll ever see. It might call itself Africa, but it acts nothing like it. The island and mainland are separated by stretches of water that plunge for miles, and that chasm creates an unthinkable difference. The fauna and flora on the island are so remarkably unusual they can only be described as otherworldly.

Madagascar is a place of spare parts, an amalgam of cultures so curious that you can't remember any more what you were supposed to see or feel or smell. You're assaulted by newness. The unfamiliar, vibrant countenance is a bit haunting, sure. It lingers. It tingles. But like the accident on the side of the road, you're compelled to stop and watch. You cannot possibly forget it.

When nightfall came, we were near Trafalgar. That day alone, we'd traveled thirty-six miles across lavish valleys and green rice paddies.

The sun was hot in the sky, scorching down in sincere, straight rays. We deviated a little from our path—a mere six miles—and ended up in a peaceful pocket of land. We decided to treat ourselves to a hotel that night, which sounds much more extravagant than it really was. You have to understand, Madagascar is not a wealthy country, so when you say hotel, it's just a very bare-bones place. Kind of like a hut in a camp-ground setting. No electricity. No comforts, and you're pretty much guaranteed bed bugs. And the shower in another hut is just a can with some water spilling out of it. But it's still a roof over your head—and for us it was one night where we didn't have to set up our tent and fetch firewood.

We unpacked a clean set of clothes and went to eat dinner at a little restaurant just a few hundred yards away. The aromas were enticing. Fondue and raclette were on the menu. The owner of the place was a French guy. He pulled up a seat at our table and started telling us all about the folklore of the island, everything from voodoo to black magic. I was fascinated by it, but Nicole was nodding off in the corner.

She leaned over, gave me a kiss on the cheek, and said she was going to go back, take a shower, and head to bed.

"Fine, fine," I said. "I'll see you in a bit," and I sat there at the table for another half hour listening to this guy telling his stories. On the road, I was always thirsty for conversation, eager to hear someone else's side of the story.

I thought nothing of Nicole heading back at the time. Why would I? When you're attempting to do something so monumental as to run the world, you see danger only in the big things. In the possibilities that truly scare you. Knives at your throat. Thieves at your door. War in your pathway. And so, without thinking a thing of it, I let her go. I had no idea, of course, that what would happen next would forever change our journey and our lives.

I got up and walked to the hut where the showers were.

"Nicole?" I said.

At first I was calm. I reassured myself that I was overreacting. She

The 25,000 Mile Love Story

was fine. Of course, she was fine. But no one answered.

"Nicole?" I said again, my voice a little louder this time than before, the first hint of fear teasing itself to the surface.

The shower curtains hung loosely in lines, inadequately covering the spaces. They were grimy on the edges, overused like old slips. On the far right I could hear water pounding onto the stones, and then I saw a pair of a women's feet peeking out below the soiled curtain.

"Nicole!" I yelled it this time. I walked toward the shower, my heart beating in strong bursts, hoping the water was just too loud for her to hear. Hoping she was just taking extra time in the shower to unwind.

I whipped the curtain open. I didn't know the face. It was a stranger.

I apologized clumsily, my words caking on my tongue. I could feel the sweat clamming up, small pools developing on my brow and palms.

In times like these, you imagine the worst. The world is full of tremendous beauty, but it also has its Hydra's head looming. The rates of rapes, kidnappings, and murders flooded to the front of my head. There is a risk to being in a foreign land. You can never really know when danger is lurking around the corner. In all of my years, and in all of my experiences, never had I been as terrified as at that moment.

I barreled back out, racing across the grounds, yelling her name loudly, hearing it echo and escape down nooks and crannies. Heads poked out, curious as to who was yelling, and why. But none of them belonged to the one person I wanted to see.

I returned to our hut, praying we had just missed each other along the path. And, for a second, as I entered the doorway, I was swallowed up in relief. She was there. My chest heaved out, blood started flowing through my veins again. Thank God, I repeated in my head.

But, just as soon as I had exhaled, I took in the full picture. She was there, yes, but she wasn't moving. Her limbs were entirely stiff and immobile. Her eyes were rolled back into her head. I couldn't tell if her heart was beating.

It happens many times every second in Africa. Something goes dreadfully wrong, caused by the deadliest critter on the continent. But you don't know it yet. And you won't know it for a week or two. You'll go on as though it's any other day, with solid health and a sturdy backbone. The signs still aren't visible. And there's no reason to suspect it's happened.

It starts with a bite. Something so simple, so painless, that you don't think another thing of it. If somebody asked you, chances are you wouldn't even be sure when it happened. But happen it did. The mosquito, that wry little creature, comes when least expected—eyeing a bare plot of skin to sink into. She rears up, nods her head down, and plunges her long mouth into the skin, piercing the flesh. She sinks through the skin, then a sheet of fat, to hit her desired goldmine. And then she begins to drink. But the mosquito doesn't simply intake. In her constant generosity, she gives back. To keep the blood from massing into a solid, she doses the area with her saliva, which is filled with seemingly trivial, worm-like creatures. And these creatures, these tiny, almost impossibly small beings, are the malaria parasites. While fifty thousand could squish into a speck of dust, only a baker's dozen coddle their way into the bloodstream. But that's plenty. After all, it only takes one to be deadly, so deadly that an African child dies every single minute from the bite of a mosquito.

The mosquito—a wiry character with piebald wings—is the lone insect that is able to shelter and transmit the human malaria parasite. And the guilty party is always a female. Males, oddly, take no notice of the blood, while the females, in contrast, rely on the blood to nourish their mosquito babies-to-be.

Once in the bloodstream, the parasites scurry on to do their dirty work, heading down to the liver where each individual parasite tunnels itself into a separate liver cell, making itself quite at home. On the outside of the human body, everything seems fine, rosy. But inside, the parasites are setting up business. They are throwing open doors and laying out artillery. And they are multiplying at a terrifying rate. They digest all of a cell's healthy, original contents, and bulge out explosively with their dirt and their filth. Each cell has replicated itself no less than 40,000 times. It's no longer a whisper, but a yell. It is pandemonium, and it now sets loose into the streets, swimming down the blood stream and through the circulatory system. But still, they aren't satisfied. They are growing. And they will keep multiplying with an endurance you wish you had yourself.

And this is when you begin to understand that your body is not your own any more. Something has happened. Something strange and drastically wrong. There are physical signs. Your temperature starts to rise. You have headaches, muscle pains, fever. You shiver, you sweat. You're cold, hot, sticky. You are uncomfortable. But more than that, you are already defeated. No matter what your body tries to do to cope, to shake them out, they only keep multiplying. There are billions of them.

In the worst situations, some of the infected cells skirt the thin blood vessels of the brain and bolt on. And this bond is the death knell. It causes the brain to swell and the malaria, which was already traumatic, has risen and manifested itself in a new way—cerebral malaria. There is nothing you could fear more. And at this point, the body falls apart completely. The parasites have ravaged so much of what is good, that there are no healthy cells left to do the fighting. You can hardly breathe or pump blood. Brain cells die. You struggle, quiver and, finally, spill headfirst, thrashing, into a coma—a welcome reprieve from the madness.

This was one of our biggest concerns before leaving on the journey, the inevitable sickness. In Switzerland—and for that matter, in most well-developed countries—we don't have to worry about the insects and the death they carry around in their tiny clinches, ready, at any moment, to inject. It's the affliction of the underprivileged. So easy to overlook. So easy to view as just an everyday reality of the unprosperous. Their lives are literally governed, and eliminated, by the tiny army. In an age of such progress and advancement, malaria now touches more people than it ever has before, running rife in 106 nations, threatening no less than half the world's people. In a disquieting statistic, the number of malaria deaths each year may have been greatly miscalculated. According to a study published by the journal Lancet, in 2004, there were actually 1.24 million deaths from malaria worldwide—practically double what the World Health Organization reported.

And it's this fact that malaria can't be contained and is so widespread, which is so terrifying. The heady strains so resistant to the drugs thrown up against it that it can hardly be controlled. It is a mastermind of death. A fatal pile up with no end. Just now, in this very year, the little mosquito will pierce the exposed flesh of a billion people, and a million individuals—mothers, fathers, daughters, brothers, sisters, husbands, and wives—will become a common statistic, an expected tombstone.

The disease is not new. It is legendary. It has grown over the millennia through the wisdom of its experiences—finding the loopholes in our vulnerabilities so that it can stick around with us a little while longer, invading and defeating our immune systems. Few nations have survived it, and no individual has been too great to succumb to it—including the famed Hippocrates and Alexander the Great. The disease itself finds its roots in the Italian word *mal'aria*, translated literally to "bad air." The disease swept up the cobblestones of Rome, lingering for centuries. Four popes fell to it, as did the poet Dante. It may very well have halted the armies of two of the most legendary warriors, Attila the Hun and Genghis Khan. It swept, too, through the United States, putting its prongs in George Washington, Abraham Lincoln, and Ulysses S. Grant. Indeed, in the 1800s, the disease became so rampant that a physician was petitioned to construct an enormous wire screen around the perimeter of Washington, D.C. in the name of safety. There are scientists who avidly believe that half of the population that has ever lived has fatally succumbed to the bite.

But the thirsty disease hasn't settled at humans. Malaria has spiked its way in stealthily, defeating the immune systems of mice, birds, porcupines, monkeys, bats, and snakes.

It is a malaria-saturated planet, and now it had come to my household.

I was standing in the doorway of our hut, very near her poor body, not knowing what to do, when the seizures began. Nicole started thrashing about on the floor, as though she were tired of her own limbs and wished to rid herself of them.

Her whole body convulsed, her tongue flip-flopping about her mouth with no signs of control or restraint. It was as though, in the blink of an eye, she had come to life, only no life I had ever seen her in before. Writhing back and forth, she howled, her voice at a pitch so high and loud it was wolf-like. How could a tiny, beautiful person make a sound so terrifying to the human ear? For the first time on the trip, I was scared. And, for the briefest of moments, the fear paralyzed me. I didn't recognize my wife.

The most terrifying things in life are those you can't see coming. The situations that hijack an average day and put you in shoes you'd always heard about but never actually stood in yourself. I'd known people who had lost spouses, and men who had to watch their wives wither away, day by day, taken by cancer. I'd known mountain guides and their clients who had perished. I'd known people who'd lost their loved ones in a car accident, their bodies plowed over by some renegade at the wheel who'd slammed through a red-light. I'd seen their grief and how it cocooned their whole body. But things like that didn't happen to me. And certainly not to Nicole.

She was fine when she had left the dinner table for the shower. She had mentioned no pain, no sickness. She had just smiled and said she was off to the shower, perhaps a little fatigued, but nothing to cause alarm. But then this? And so quickly? When I got back to our hut, I found Nicole on the floor and thought she was dead, lying there listlessly. Moments later, she was spitting out what were trying to be words, but her voice was coarse and hateful. She was sweating, spinning. She had no control over herself.

I had no idea then what was really happening, that her fever had reached maximum intensity. That her body was practically boiling itself. She was trying to fight it off as best she could, but the damage had already been done. One, perhaps two weeks ago, it had started with a bite. In the middle of the night, a mosquito had stolen a sweet drink, and that one little moment had erupted into this.

I started screaming. Some people ran over from the restaurant. The owner helped me lift Nicole from the floor to the bed. She had to go to the hospital. We all knew this. But even in her delirious state, Nicole fought the idea. She was adamant about not going, throwing a tantrum like a five-year-old child, slamming down her wrists and curdling her words. She was scared of the injections. And whether her mind was really stable or not, I couldn't blame her.

When we're at home in Switzerland, there's a sense of reliability and security. Sure, we might not know exactly what this shot is or that pill is, or how it can help, but there's a bit of faith that the men in the white coats with the heavily chicken-scratched charts know just what it is that they're doing. At home, there are regulations and protocols and degrees pinned to the wall in mahogany frames. Here, there's a man who barely speaks English who looks like he hasn't slept in three days. Here, yes, he could make things better, but he could also make things much, much worse.

But at that point, I didn't see that we had a choice. We put Nicole in the car. The capital, Antananarivo, was fifty miles away, which was no less than three hours by four-wheel drive, under the best of conditions. It was a dirty, bumpy road, hardly paved, and that night it was raining hard. We slipped all over the road, and all the while Nicole was shaking and trembling. I couldn't help but think she was crazy and that she would never recover. How does someone come back from something like that?

As I tried to hold her arms down to keep her from punching the side of the car, I thought, if she makes it through this, I'll be happy, of course. But, if she makes it through this and stays like this, it's probably worse. This is no way to live.

We finally got her to the hospital. Even though there were a few in town, only one would accept her—a U.S. military hospital—and likely that was the best anyway. People were swarming about Nicole, staring at her as though she were under a microscope. Doctors. Nurses. Interns. Anesthesiologists. We were jammed inside a room in the hospital, starched white with a single rolling bed and medical equipment that looked like it was inherited from the 1980s. The medical staff tied down her arms, binding them at the wrists, and then covered her hands in mitts so she wouldn't be able to hurt anyone, including herself. Nicole was panicked, though I think to her it was also just a gray fog, a state of being where she couldn't quite put her finger on what was actually happening and what she thought was happening. Test after test was taken. With tubes flowing in and out of her, shots sent into her system with regularity, she was a reluctant guinea pig. We spent the better part of the day with an overwhelming feeling of uncertainty, but Nicole had always been a fighter. I reassured myself of this. If my wife was anything, she was determined. She was strong-minded and gritty. She would get in the trenches with anyone and anything.

The answers didn't come from the hospital. We stayed overnight, Nicole regained her composure and a little bit of her confidence, and we left, told that it was just an episode. A manic fever that had run amok.

"Rest and she'll be better," they promised us. And since we wanted to believe them, we did. But Nicole wasn't getting better. It didn't take long to see that. Her thoughts weren't right. She'd talk, piecing together whole thoughts, but they wouldn't make any sense. She was speaking like a lunatic. And she was extremely anxious. About everything.

For a few days, we stayed with a friend we had met there—Anta, a Madagascan delegate of a humanitarian association. She set Nicole up as comfortably as she could. She made up a makeshift bed in the living room, tucked between end tables and wooden vases. She piled on blankets that Nicole shrugged on and off throughout the nights, fluctuating between hot sweats and cold spells. After a seizure, a person is in a dramatically reduced state of awareness; the reflexes are rubbed raw. There's no sense of composure, just a bumbling condition of bare consciousness.

I sat up by Nicole's side throughout the nights, while she tried to sleep. Her seizures and fits lasted three hours or more, and then they would finally subside. What remained was a frail and wilted version of my wife. They exhausted her. She was caked in sweat and looked remarkably dehydrated. Anta came into the room frequently, her tiny body hovering above Nicole, a protective little hummingbird. She thought we should go to the hospital; I knew this. But she respected our wishes, doing what she could to make the situation bearable.

Nicole was coming around. And when she'd get a break from the seizures, she'd let loose about her worries. Just how serious is this? Will I make it through the night? Will I fully recover? Will episodes like this happen again? Frequently? What is wrong with me?

After a few days, I took her to have her head examined. The doctors had to have missed something—something that was causing her life to be so erratic.

The test results came in: the brain lacked tone following the coma. The most probable diagnosis, the doctor said, was cerebral malaria. The seizures, apparently, like the ones Nicole had been having, would continue. For years. Gradually, they would peter out. But not soon.

We sank back in the chairs. Cerebral malaria. I repeated the words over and over again in my mind, letting the diagnosis sink in. It was a punch to the gut. And a bit maddening really. How does one move forward from something like this? How does one really recover? Does one ever? And then without looking at me, as if in answer, Nicole put her hand in mine. Not out of worry or out of fear, I could tell. But out of strength. Like she was telling me with a firm squeeze of her hand that while we were susceptible to the unknown, we could also fight it.

CHAPTER NINETEEN

The Seizures

"Although the world is full of suffering, it is full also of the overcoming of it."

—Helen Keller

It's not unusual to lose people in this kind of life we've chosen. When you step off your porch, it's always touch and go, no matter how prepared you think you are, how many teams of people are behind you, or how many forms of technology are tracing you. Sometimes there simply isn't room for precautions—and if there is, sometimes they're just not enough.

Nicole and I both knew, before we left, that something bad could happen. Or, better put, likely would happen. The odds were not in our favor. Forget about the physical element for a moment—the wear and tear 25,000 miles takes on the joints and muscles, how plugging away mile after mile, day after day, can deteriorate a body, ripping it not only of its fervor, but its ability. Forget about how long, solitary stretches in a dry desert, nights without a bed, and weeks without communication can strip your mind of its calm and serenity and resolve. There are other things that can break you down on this kind of journey. There's the human element. The war and famine and poverty. The disease. The robbery and slander and threats.

If all you focused on in every opportunity were the number of ways it could go wrong, you could talk yourself out of doing anything. My, the world is full of landmines! But that's why you've got to pause. Keep perspective. Sure, there are risks when you join the road, venturing out beyond your square of comfort. And you don't know which ones will greet you, soiling your hopes. Maybe none. Maybe all. It's a vulnerable landscape. But, in it you stand not only to lose everything, but also to gain it.

Nobody knows that better than the running man. People knew him as a lot of things. Caballo Blanco. White Horse. Micah True. But whatever you called him, Michael Randall Hickman—a pure, long-distance runner of a marvelous, mythical nature—understood what it was to live intimately in the present, risking and inevitably losing it all.

It was odd, the manner in which he disappeared. People, in a way, sort of always expected he would go in a dramatic flair, cast off into Mexico's steep and treacherous Copper Canyons by one ill placement of the foot. No matter how many times you run those hills, no matter how your feet learn to mold and move against the shifty shape of land, it is never as predictable as you would like. In that landscape, it is far easier to fail than to succeed. Caballo Blanco lived a dangerous life in the Mexican Outback, one where faith and joy outweighed the risks of bandits, deadly cliffs, and drug lords. He loved running—he believed it could and did change his life. And he lived this happy, almost released existence among the legendary Tarahumara Indians, buried deep in the pockets of the Copper Canyons. And it's in this reclusive existence that he felt most at home.

He first met the Tarahumara in 1993 at the Leadville Trail 100 Run—a race of one hundred miles in the Colorado Rockies, with elevations tiering from 9,200 to 12,600 feet. It's the type of race where you learn to respect the land and where hundreds of runners, who thought they were built out of infinite endurance, are tested and humbled. The Tarahumara were running and the gangly, memorable form of Michael Randall Hickman—who would become the unforgettable Caballo Blanco—volunteered to pace them for the last half of the trail.

As it turns out, much like me, Caballo was an ex-professional boxer.

His body, fit from years of training, was well toned for the daring landscape. And the running not only healed his body, but his heart—one that had been sorely broken. He wandered the Colorado trails for miles and miles searching for an answer that would bring resolution and peace to his mind. And that night, running with the legendary Tarahumara, he sensed a great deal of relief. There was wisdom in their running, he understood. Wisdom in their pace, grace, and solitude. And so he decided, in his search for truth, to follow after them—changing his name to Micah True, and then, for the children's pleasure, Caballo Blanco—a stomping figure of mirth and speed that would plow through their villages, prompting giggles and delight. The Tarahumara had a secret, he always said. A secret of motion. As humans, in our busy state, we've forgotten that we're supposed to be creatures of motion. And, if we sit still and confine ourselves long enough, we'll begin to suffer what any caged animal suffers. In other words, as author Chris McDougall says, "The Tarahumara aren't smarter than us. They've just got better memories." And in that way, he lived among them for nearly two decades—remembering the right things.

The disappearance of Caballo was not an unexpected thing. He would hightail it off for days and weeks, carving out paths in the forgotten land for the sheer pleasure of it. He wouldn't tell anyone when he would leave or when he would come back, so his presence was always a surprise, an unexpected amusement.

But this time, the peculiar thing was that he was expected. He was in Gila, New Mexico, and told a friend he'd be back before mid-day, leaving his dog behind. Then, he went a mere three miles down the road into an American wilderness park—hardly the terrifying landscape he normally pounded through—and was gone. Just like that.

Word of Caballo's disappearance came quickly, and it spread through the ranks of his friends and admirers. Scott Jurek, Kyle Scaggs, Chris McDougall, and Peter Sarsgaard all flocked to New Mexico, desperate to find the friend they hoped they hadn't permanently lost. Teams were sent out with pictures of Caballo's shoe tread. Over one hundred individuals joined the search—using helicopters, horses, dog teams, and even Caballo's personal running club—the Mas Locos.

His body was inevitably found in a deserted canyon, about a mile southeast of the Gila Cliff Dwellings. He was lying near a cold stream, his legs half-immersed in water with a half full water bottle sitting next to him, as though he were entirely at peace. If he had to go, the place was perfect. He was even led out of the canyon on a White Horse named Tequila.

To many, in a way, Caballo always felt mythical—a human creature who could endure and overcome anything, somehow missing the land mines that would always befall others. And, so, his death, so mysterious and gentle in nature, confounds, and it reminds us that the risk is real. And, I would imagine Caballo would say worth it.

I looked at the clock. It had been two hours. This made me worry. We were in Melbourne, Australia. We'd rented a hotel for a couple of nights to recoup, and Nicole had decided to go out to the supermarket to grab some food.

"I'll be quick," she said. "Don't worry." But this was a silly thing to say. I knew, as she knew, that it could happen at any moment.

The first doctor we'd seen in Madagascar had been right. There was nothing we could do. Nicole would recover year after year, a little bit at a time. But very slowly. Painfully slow. He promised the seizures would eventually become shorter and more spread out and then, sometime very far down the road, they might disappear altogether. This was the best-case scenario, though. We had to be realistic.

We tried a few different treatments, but none of them took. Possibly because Nicole didn't take to them either. She was stubborn.

"It is what it is," she'd say. And when I'd push her, she'd fight back. "I'm strong. I'll make it through this. Shut up and keep going." Then in a few hours or the next day or really whenever it felt like it, another seizure would creep up, and she'd be on her back writhing.

The risk was no longer just real to us. It was present.

I checked the clock again. Now, two and a half hours. Something had to have happened. And I had a good feeling what. I got in a taxi and headed to the nearest hospital. I walked in the front doors of the ER and spoke with a pretty, pale-faced woman who was clacking on her keyboard with her red fingernails.

"Excuse me," I said. "But have you had a woman by the name of Nicole Roetheli check in recently?"

The woman looked up at me and then back down to her keyboard, typing away.

"Why yes, we have. About half an hour ago."

Nicole, as it turns out, had made it to the supermarket. But, somewhere between the chocolate and the spaghetti, she'd had a seizure. And, not knowing what to do or where she belonged, the people around her had taken her to the hospital straight away.

If only I had a dollar for every time that had happened.

On the road, when Nicole would start to feel bad, she'd pull the bike onto the side of the road, her hands already twitching. Then she'd lie down on the side of the road, I'd bring over the bedroll and try to make a place comfortable for her. And then, as if on cue, she'd start to shake and scream. It would last anywhere from ten minutes to forty minutes. And I'd just sit there the whole time, rather helpless. Then, when she was done, she'd take ten seconds, stand up, and say, "I'm fine. We can keep going." And she'd say it as though nothing at all had happened. We'd keep running down the road, and then we'd do it all over again a couple hours later or whenever the next wave would hit.

As you can imagine, everywhere we went, we caused quite a scene. Before it all happened, we already stood out on the road. I mean, I was a guy in shorts running next to a woman on a motorbike with a trailer. We were the odd couple for sure. But after the seizures started, we drew flocks. When Nicole would shake on the street, we'd have a hundred people around us all at once. In India, forget it. And everyone would come with new advice.

People all the time would tell us to go home. They thought we were absurd to keep going in this state. But Nicole didn't want to go home. She wanted to finish.

"I have the condition here, or I have it there," she'd say. "What difference does it make?"

And I had to agree she had a point.

The worst came in Nepal. It was about a year after the seizures had started, but in Kathmandu they were breaking like waves on the shore.

I hadn't seen them that bad since the first night in Madagascar. I had a friend there with me who was a mountain guide.

He'd come over with some customers to do some climbing, and when he saw Nicole, he couldn't believe her condition.

"You have to go home," he said. "At the very least, you need to have her checked out by a specialist and see if anything can be done."

I agreed, but convincing Nicole was another matter entirely. There was a part of her that felt deep inside that if she got on a plane, she might never come back. But inevitably her health got so bad, it demanded it. But then it wasn't easy finding a seat on the rare flights to Europe, because with the political turmoil, a state of siege had been declared in Nepal. Finally, a couple already booked on the plane, was kind enough to give up their seats, and we were headed back to Switzerland in just a matter of days.

Nicole spent ten days in the hospital in Sion, and the whole time I slept on the floor right by her side. She felt so vulnerable and tiny. Her family and my family flocked around her, trying to be supportive, but I could tell it hurt her to be home. Sure, she wanted to come back to her family and friends, but under other conditions.

The doctors took test after test, scanning her everywhere. The malaria was clearly having massive effects on her body. She lacked iron and vitamins. She suffered from anemia. It seemed to be crisis after crisis. But none so big that they were insurmountable. All of her vitals were stable. And while the doctors fretted, they came back with the same conclusion: there is nothing that can be done. The best medicine is time.

Nicole's mother stood at the head of the bed, stroking her hair.

"My dear daughter," she said. "I want you to take to the road again, because it's your whole life. I wouldn't want that to change for anything."

And somehow, miraculously, a mother's words had a healing effect that evaded medicine. We were able to return to Nepal a few days later. While the seizures continued, Nicole's overall health was on the rise.

Things were looking up!

CHAPTER TWENTY

The Boa

"Some people talk to animals. Not many listen though. That's the problem."

—A.A. Milne

One of our first nights in Madagascar after Nicole's cerebral malaria attacks, we were invited by a farmer to set up our tent for the night on his land. And, fortunately for us, he had a menagerie of animals. Madagascar is rich in wildlife. Crazy configurations of lizards and amphibians you couldn't cook up in your wildest imagination. This farmer in particular had a ton of lizards and iguanas, gigantic creatures as large as beach balls.

Nicole and I spent the afternoon walking around looking at the different animals, and the farmer came up to us after a while, noticing our curiosity.

"You like the animals, do you?" he asked.

Nicole and I nodded vigorously, thanking him again for letting us peek about his property.

"Well, if you like those," he said, "I've got a boa constrictor that you will want to see. If you'd like, I can bring him around, you can put him on your arms, and your wife can take a picture. Would you like that?"

But, of course. How could I turn that down?

The farmer skirted around the house, and Nicole and I waited patiently. I knew almost nothing about snakes though, which would prove to be unfortunate.

Finally, he brought the snake, curled around his arm, and it was immense. Nearly six and a half feet long, and it was a solid thirty pounds. I never imagined a snake could be so heavy. It was the first time I had one on my arms.

And immediately, just as soon as the farmer had handed him to me, the snake began rapidly turning around my right arm. And after about thirty seconds or so, he began to squeeze. Knowing as little as I did, I had no idea what to do, and I began to panic. The pressure was building, and that's when I made a huge mistake.

While I had the snake wrapping his body around my right arm, I had his neck and head in my left hand. And when I began to panic, I squeezed my left hand on instinct. Naturally, the boa didn't take too kindly to that, and he leapt toward my face defensively, sinking his teeth into my eyelid, where two punctures went straight through. And, with his tail, he proceeded to lash open my cheek. Blood began pouring out, and Nicole, out of fright, knocked over the tripod and came running toward me. The farmer, on the other hand, went running the other way.

The blood didn't clot for some time, but in the end, everything was all right. No poison, just a black eye and a good lesson about boas.

I looked at Nicole and smiled.

"This was my last boxing match," I said. "And I lost."

CHAPTER TWENTY-ONE

Holy Land

"What makes the desert beautiful,' said the little prince, 'is that some-where it hides a well...."

—Antoine de Saint-Exupery

Coco Chanel, the famed French designer, once said that before leaving the house for the day, a woman should stop and look in the mirror, then choose one piece of jewelry to take off. The principle was unfussy, but true: simplify.

We live in a century of excess. All around there is so much to dis-tract and occupy us, so much to acquire, that the places which cause us to scale back are north stars, guiding us in the right direction.

There is no place with greater simplistic truth than the desert. It is honest and straightforward about both its dangers and delights.

The Sinai Peninsula is shaped like a triangle and juts out between the Mediterranean Sea to the north and the Red Sea to the south. It is the only portion of Egypt that is located in Asia rather than Africa, so it serves as a bridge between the two.

When our feet hit the Sinai desert, it was already a vast canvas of gray sand, as far as the eye could see. It was October of 2001, and the heat was unrelenting. Most people flock to the coasts when they come to the Sinai. They swim in the waters so clear and piercingly cool. But, they miss the great expanse, the place where Moses and the Hebrew people wandered the desert for forty years searching for the Promised Land.

The Sinai is a point of convergence for the continents and a place of separation for the seas. It is mountainous and arid. There's something terrifying about it. During the day, the heat here is overwhelming; at night, it's bitterly cold.

Few human beings live in the desert. Aside from the cities on the coast, the peninsula is inhabited by a Bedouin community that survives thanks to palm trees and date palms. They band together around water sources. Mythical and alluring figures, the Bedouins are the lords of the sands. They are also breeders of sheep, black goats, and dromedaries. In winter, they host tourists, or they go farther off to cultivate vegetables, oranges, and dates. The oil fields and road construction also offer some possibilities for work. The children go to school for two to three years, after which they help their parents, primarily by selling jewelry. During this time, the women care for the herds.

But these people are few and far between. Unlike India and Bangladesh, in the desert there were no sounds, no traffic. The only thing I heard was my breathing and the hum of Nicole's motorcycle. All was quiet on the Sinai front. The miles each day climbed on top of one another in similar fashion; none were very distinct. It was an odd feeling to run toward nowhere, to have no landmark but the horizon, which kept receding into the sand. Imagine standing in a white room all day long, waking up in it the next, and staring at it again. Then repeat this week after week. You would begin to lose track of yourself, track of where you were, and how fast things were happening. If you can imagine that, you can imagine a fraction of the desert.

It was easy for Nicole to drive there, which was a plus. There was nothing in her way, no bumps in the road or traffic to navigate. But for me, the heat made it arduous. I took sips of Coca Cola all day long. The mercury fluctuated in the triple digits. My throat cracked, my brain boiled. Step after step, I dreamed of forests, canopies, rivers, oceans, lakes, valleys, flowerbeds.

What must Moses and his people have felt like?

In the desert, you look for the slightest bit of change. Just a shift in the scenery that will let you know you're not losing your mind and that you actually are, despite your worries, making progress. Even if it's the smallest detail. A slightly different color of sand, perhaps. Or an unexplained rock. But really, there's no bit of life out there. There are a few twigs here and there that painfully try to keep growing, but the sun beats down so hard and so fast that it sucks the life right out of them.

For miles and miles and miles, it's de-energizing, painfully barren. But then, just as you feel like you're going to lose it, something glorious opens up: the sunset.

Here and there, Nicole and I would find a spot in the desert that was like a refuge, particularly when we came to the mountains: Mount Moses and Mount Saint Catherine. Unlike the rest of the desert, nothing about the mountains was uniform or monotonous.

The first night we were there at the campsite, I lit my pipe. The sun coasted over the top of the peaks in bright pinks and yellows and reds, and the twilight glanced its head out slowly. In those moments, the silence didn't bother me; it nourished me. Is this what people find in religion? I wondered. An oasis that springs out of nowhere, something that provides beauty and solace in a barren land.

My daughter, Clara, turned sixteen that day. I sent up a wish for her and was reminded, once again, that there is a price we pay for our dreams. I missed my children dearly.

While the running was unbelievably demanding, I loved the desert for its history and for its quiet.

The Saint Catherine monastery is nestled at the bottom of the valley, at an altitude of 1,500 meters (4,921 feet). It lies at the mouth of a gorge at the foot of Mount Sinai. It's one of the oldest and most enduring Christian monasteries in the world. According to the folklore, Catherine of Alexandria was a Christian martyr who was sentenced to death on the wheel. But when the wheel was unsuccessful, they moved to behead her. The legends say angels flew her relics to Mount Sinai, and around the year 800, monks found her remains. Though people know it as Saint Catherine's, the full name is the Sacred and Imperial Monastery of the God-Trodden Mount of Sinai.

And Mount Sinai itself, whew! What a story! There are two routes up to the summit. The longer and perhaps easier is the Siket El Bashait, which takes about two and half hours on foot. The steeper route, though, is the Siket Sayidna Musa—3,750 "steps of penitence" which go straight to the top, and which were cut into the rock by the monks.

At the summit of the mountain there is a mosque that is still currently used by Muslims. There is also a Greek Orthodox chapel, which was built on the ruins of a sixteenth century church. This part you can't venture into. Moses is said to have received the Tablets of Law inscribed with the Ten Commandments there.

I trekked up the 3,750 steps and watched the sun set. Yes, indeed. It was holy land.

As we approached the end of our journey through the Sinai—12,065 kilometers (7,497 miles) down—we took a wrong turn. In the desert, that can be costly, but for us it was a blessing. We met Mary Magdalene, a nun who lives in the twisting paths of the valleys. She was covered in a long, black tunic and had a white cloth wrapped around her head. She leaned heavily on her staff, her age showing.

Sister Mary Magdalene had been a recluse, all alone in the desert, for seventeen years. With her own hands and from the native granite stones, she constructed her little chapel, as well as her house.

"It does get lonely sometimes," she said reluctantly, as though solitude of such a kind was not allowed to weigh on a person. She was full of whispers from the desert, stories of the Bedouin, of death and romance. Her eyes were bright and dancing; I'm not sure if she'd had that much pleasure in years.

Twice a month, she walks as far as the village of Saint Catherine, where she buys provisions. And that's where we met her, on the road there. I offered to fill up her bag with enough food to last her for a month, and then I asked her if I could carry it.

She stopped, surprised and quite moved. In the span of seventeen years, in the very Holy Land that it is, that was the first time someone had ever made her that offer.

Serge Running the World

Running in the winds and rains of hurricanes (three) in SE USA.

Crossing a river—a tricky event.

Running in the desert with no landmarks on horizon.

Treacherous footing doesn't slow Serge.

Nicole Riding her Motorcycle Around the World

Nicole riding in the snow and cold.

It's slippery up here! Will I pass the driving test?

The "joys" of riding in the rain and wind of hurricane Charley.

How deep is this water? Driving through flood waters.

Bike and trailer turned over—not the only time on the World Tour.

Serge Running the Roads of the World

Running among the endless trucks of India—danger & pollution.

Running through a flooded road in Australia.

Even the cows are curious about Serge running!

Special Moments on the World Tour

Serge drinking warm, curded camel milk in the Sahara Desert!

Serge Loved Nepal despite very challenging running conditions.

Serge running near the great pyramids of Egypt!

Family and friends greet Serge & Nicole at the Eiffel Tower.

The 25,000 Mile Love Story

Life on the Road

Nicole—the girl who'd never camped a day in her life before meeting Serge.

Serge & Nicole "efficiently" warming over a small fire.

Coffee heating in an open fire—a daily routine.

Repacking the trailer—AGAIN!

Life on the Road

Traveling the rocky road isn't easy.

Serge chasing mosquitos—Africa's most deadly animal.

Family escaping civil strife in Africa.

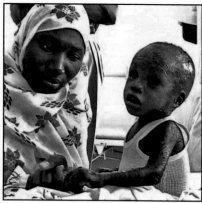

Poverty—the way too many of the world's people live.

The 25,000 Mile Love Story

Dangers on the Roads of the World

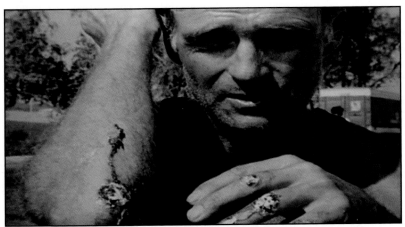

Serge's arm after hit-and-run vehicle struck him in India.

Competition for the road in Bangladesh—how can I get through?

Consuming dust-pollution almost daily on the road.

Civil unrest in Africa—encountered numerous times on World Tour.

Health Issues on the World Tour

Nicole suffered frequent seizures from malaria during the last 40 months of the World Tour.

Suffering from dehydration and exhaustion—the consequences of running in extreme heat and humidity.

COURSE AUTOUR DU GLOBE

RUN FOR KIDS

Nicole Roetheli hospitalisée

Partis jeudi de Katmandou, Serge et Nicole Roetheli ont atterri dans la nuit de vendredi à samedi à Cointrin. Motif, Nicole Roetheli souffre de violentes crises de paludisme et est soignée pour l'instant à l'hôpital de Sion.

Les Roetheli ont donc stoppé momentanément la course autour du globe en faveur de Terres des hommes. **PAGE 11**

Nicole returns to Swiss hospital for care due to cerebral malaria.

Serge with Boa—Serge lost this "round" with bite to eye lid.

The Beauty of Nature
Witnessed Along the Roads of the World

The beauty of an African sunset.

Sunset in the mountains.

Serge running a jungle path along the border of Mali and Guinea.

More Beauty from Around the World

12 Apostles Rocks just off southern Australian coast.

Gorgeous Iguaza Falls—Argentina, Brazil, Paraguay border.

Serge climbed Mt. Aconcugua—highest in the Americas (22,831 ft.).

Major Man-Made Structures

Taj Mahal—extravagance among so much poverty in India.

How did they get those stones up there on the Pyramids of Egypt?

Passing the famous Sidney Opera House.

Statue of Jesus towering over Rio de Janeiro.

Man-Made Structures

Nicole is fascinated by U.S. Capitol and Mall.

Reunion with friends at World Trade Center ruins.

Nicole jostles for space with "cabbies" on Fifth Avenue, NYC.

Statue of Liberty—a symbol of freedom & opportunity.

Dangerous Animal Encounters on the World Tour

Encountering mama and baby elephant in Thailand—danger?

Lion "greets" Serge and Nicole at roadside—Whoa!

Hippo—Africa's second-deadliest animal.

Sedate Animal Encounters

One of many sacred cows in India.

Nicole greeting a fellow traveler.

Camels—beasts of burden in the desert.

Unexpected visitors—parrots on the motorcycle in Australia.

Interesting Human Encounters

Painted Indian forehead—a different culture.

Painted body of man from India.

African lady carrying water on her head and child on her back.

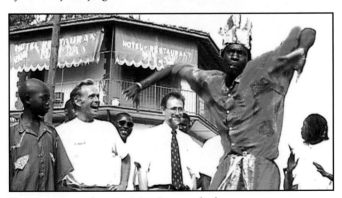

Dancer in Senegal entertaining Serge and others.

The Finish Line—Saillon, Switzerland, May 7, 2005

An emotional Serge & Nicole at the finish line.

The exhilaration—25,422 miles completed!

CHAPTER TWENTY-TWO

Caged Bird

"The caged bird sings with a fearful trill, of things unknown, but longed for still, and his tune is heard on the distant hill, for the caged bird sings of freedom."

—Maya Angelou

Prior to leaving for the World Tour, I met with our charitable foundation to plan some visits across the world with humanitarian organizations that were working with kids in orphanages, hospitals, and prisons. Nicole and I both wanted to spend some actual quality time with the people we were trying to help. Unfortunately, half way through the Tour, the charitable foundation pulled out. We were given just one last stop: a jail in Lebanon with some teenagers.

It was one of the harder visits to set up, and I didn't just want to go, say I'd been there, and snap a picture. I wanted to share some quality time with the kids, really get to know them. It took months to organize but, eventually, we were granted a few hours of time with some of the juvenile inmates. The jail was located on the top of a hill, and it was very much like a scene from a Hollywood movie. The building was very old and dark, shrouded with blackness. It loomed over the hill in a frightful, menacing way. When we walked in, three metal doors clanged behind us, ceremoniously locking us in.

The place was overcrowded. I could already tell that without even having to ask, but in fact, it had three times the stated capacity. Teens, adults, and elderly people were packed into every cranny of this dismal place, almost like the peanuts crammed into a packing carton.

We played sports with the teenagers for most of the time, and I let them win. That was important, I think. You've got these kids who are told all day long that they're no good, that they can't be winners. That they've messed up and aren't redeemable, but they need to know that they've got some potential in them. That's the only way anyone will ever get better.

While I hoped to have a good connection with one of the kids, truthfully I didn't expect it. It was such a short period of time and most of those kids were too hardened to be vulnerable, but in the early afternoon, a teenager named Nadim came up to me. He was of decent build with deep olive skin and tussled brown hair. Just fourteen years old, but he was very aggressive. He wanted to talk to me, to share his story with me, I could tell that. But he didn't quite know how to do it.

I waited for him patiently. Normally I speak a lot, but this time, I knew it was best to listen.

"Do you know why I'm here?" he asked, finally.

And, of course, not knowing him at all, I said "No."

"I killed my dad," he said very powerfully, without the slightest bit of hesitation.

"And I'm proud I killed my dad."

When you hear something like that on the movies, it's good. A nice bit of drama mixed in there. But when you hear it in person, from a child, of all people, it disturbs you to your core.

"Why did you do that?" I asked.

He paused, reflecting seriously for a moment. "Because my dad raped my sister."

The world is not so black and white, is it?

The boy then got up and left, but the story haunted me. Was he a good boy, or was he a bad boy? Was he true and just? How does a story like this make sense in the bigger picture of general human decency?

When the day was over, the same boy brought me a drawing of a cage with a bird inside.

"I drew this bird in a cage because *you* are free and *I* am not. I won't be free for a long time...."

He turned around then and walked away, making a far larger impression than even he had anticipated.

After Nicole and I left the jail, we went to his hometown village the next day. I was curious about this boy and where he came from. What did the people think? It was a small village of Muslim orientation. In that kind of a culture, when a member of the family does something shameful—like the father did—the whole family has to move away from the village. They are scorned, unwanted. But when the boy killed his father—his one justice—the whole family was accepted again. Redeemed even.

I talked to people throughout the town. The boy was a hero.

Nicole and I left though with heavy hearts, clutching our bird-cage drawing with our prized possessions.

One rape, one murder, one prisoner. To us, it was the story of three tragedies.

CHAPTER TWENTY-THREE

India

"When you travel, remember that a foreign country is not designed to make you comfortable. It is designed to make its own people comfortable."

—Clifton Fadiman

The first phrase that comes to mind is "too much." Everything is simply too much. The people. The colors. The noise. The traffic. The buildings. The poverty. Everything extends until the horizon and then, somehow, continues with no end, dipping into the forever.

Before we crossed the border over to a new country, Nicole and I always prepared ourselves, both physically and mentally, for what we'd be walking into. And if there's one thing for certain about our trip, it's that India was not a country that we could treat like we had all the others. Within the first moments, it has your pulse racing.

Tucked into South Asia, India is the seventh largest country in terms of geographical area, and the second most populous country in the world, housing over 1.2 billion people. It's bounded by water, the Indian Ocean on the south, the Arabian Sea to the southwest, and the Bay of Bengal to the southeast. The land borders Pakistan, China, Nepal, Bhutan, Burma (a country that we had planned to run, but although the border guards would allow us in, they simply would not allow the motorcycle to enter), and Bangladesh.

India is a place of contradictions. A harmony of beauty and squalor. It's saddled down by three centuries of British imperialism and its own attempts to redraft its story, making what you come across complicated and perplexing, especially if you haven't been there before. On one corner of the street is a lavish five star hotel dripping in luxury; on the other is a slum so putrid and decrepit that hardly one person who lives there could cough up enough money to buy a tea pot.

We arrived first in Bombay. It was five o'clock in the morning. While the city was mostly sleeping, we had a quick wake-up call of our own. There were hundreds of people sleeping right on the ground, in the streets, in front of the buildings. They were practically naked and hanging on top of one another like clothes on a line. The double-decker buses drove through the streets. Dust coated the air. Nobody notices a mess there.

When the city woke up, it was nothing but colors. And the women, my God, they were striking. And they walked about with such dignity. Most wore their saris, the traditional Indian garment. They were graceful and joyful, majestic even. Nicole was entranced by them.

That night, we waited in a main square while our motorcycle sat in customs. It wasn't altogether a bad thing though. The problems with the motorcycle always slowed us down, but they also reminded us that we needed to stop and look around more often. People milled about us. The sun set. I took out my pipe—my one luxury item on the road—and enjoyed what might be considered a moment of peace in the most bustling metropolis. A few kids climbed up onto my knees. They were so entertained by the idea of a foreigner. A few others followed after that, and soon it became a flock. They were street children, all of them. They lived off of garbage and breathed in the fumes of pollution all day long. It was the only option they had. And yet all of the kids were full of such lightheartedness, as though they didn't realize quite yet just how hard they had it.

A petite little girl with dark, flowing hair followed Nicole down the street. She asked Nicole for her name and handed her a faded flower. And of course, my dear Nicole melted, and she bought the little girl a pack of candy.

When our motorcycle finally got through customs and we were able to start running, we finally realized the congestion of the place. How India really is just one clogged artery after another. It's not easy to force your way through with so many carts drawn by horse and hand, with so many people walking about in every direction. I darted back and forth between the vehicles and people, but Nicole had much more trouble. People didn't want to let the motorcycle through.

We headed down the road that connects Bombay to New Delhi. It was like an army set out on leave all at once. No rules. Just pushing. And there was construction, too, which didn't help a thing. Nicole called it the "corridor of death." The first day we were traveling this road, a car accident killed twenty-five people and no one seemed terribly troubled, just further frustrated by the delay. The air quality was abysmal. Smog and exhaust fumes came with every gulp. That, coupled with the insanity of traffic, made running seem like a ridiculous feat. *How can people breathe here*, I wondered.

The deeper we traveled into the belly of the country, the more we became conscious of the fact that we were dealing with a place of contradictions. We passed from richness to squalor, from ecstasy to pain. India was deeply troubling, mostly because the gap between their world and ours was so big. How do you justify such a huge difference in your mind?

Consider this: hundreds of people perform the same routine every morning at the same place, at the same moment. Scattered or aligned on the sidewalks, so many "do their business" with their butts in the air, letting their yellow-colored excrement drip in front of us without the tiniest morsel of worry or restraint. The kids candidly squat with their butts resting on their own excrement.

Or consider this: a shaggy-haired man, in rags, sat on the side of the road. His bare feet were cracked, and he held some animal intestines in his hands. And then just like that, in the blink of an eye, he shoved them into his mouth like a wolf slurping up his prey.

As the days churned on, we began to feel more and more that India wasn't a place of freedom, but rather a place of repression. The inquisitiveness of the people was heightened. We had no privacy, no door to close, no space that was off limits. Everyone stared at us as though we were a science project and they were tasked to carefully observe what was under the microscope. But they didn't just look; that would have been a relief. They touched us constantly, particularly Nicole. One night she said to me, "I no longer feel that I am a woman; I have become a vulgar piece of merchandise."

But those are the roads of India for you. Traffic, pollution, honking horns, accidents, sacred cows, thousands of pedestrians, motorcycles, bicycles, goats, monkeys, elephants, camels. Eyes watching, always watching. It is an endless charade, a country without shame or embarrassment.

It's hard to understand a way of life that is so markedly different from ours, but when you're a guest in a place, it's your obligation to try to understand.

When we got to cities and walked down the streets, we had the impression that poverty in India is endless. It's infuriating to see such destitution. But when you're on the road, you learn to conduct yourself differently when confronted with so much human distress. And in spite of all of their troubles, the people seemed to be relatively happy with their daily life. Mother Teresa once said, "In the West, we have a tendency to be profit-oriented, where everything is measured according to the results and we get caught up in being more and more active to generate results. In the East—especially in India—I find that people are more content to just be, to just sit around under a banyan tree for half a day, chatting to each other. We Westerners would probably call that wasting time. But there is value to it. Being with someone, listening without a clock and without anticipation of results, teaches us about love. The success of love is in the loving—it is not in the result of loving."

Nicole and I couldn't help but think—there are so many things to learn from watching others. No matter how much we may never be like them, there were still morsels of wisdom we could take away—life lessons for us.

The people there, too, were curious. Infamously so. They poked about us as though we were new toys. And the motorcycle and gear? It might as well have been FAO Schwarz.

They asked so many questions. They tried to understand. Sometimes when we were stopped on the side of the road, we felt like we were giving a press conference. People wanted to know why we were there, what we were doing, what we were trying to accomplish. And to make matters more difficult, only 3 percent of the indigenous Indian population speaks English and there are around four thousand unofficial dialects of their own language, so they asked questions and we answered with a lot of gestures, our arms and heads moving about, trying to make sense of something. And while all the attention was trying at times, it was also a little relieving. *India was the first country where anyone bothered to ask us why we were running.*

There were also glimpses of hope. Something brilliant in the midst of all that poverty and noise. A family gave us some rupees so we could treat ourselves to a hotel for the night. And then another man, who did not appear too well-off, paid for our lunches. The kindness was embarrassing. We felt as though we were the ones who were supposed to be helping them, and yet there they were, extending their hands.

For as much as the Indian people can be in your face and breathing down your neck, no matter how overbearing it gets, their kindness is equivalent.

Henri Michaux wrote, "In India, if you do not pray, you have lost." I can understand what he means now. Everywhere we went, every mile we passed, we were assaulted by tradition. People praying and carrying on with their rituals. And all the people looked at us with just this tinge of wonder. In the East, they viewed what we were doing as a pilgrimage, and in a place like India, there is nothing more valuable than a pilgrimage.

The vast majority of people in India are Hindus, and in Hinduism there is a pecking order to the body. The head is greater than all the rest, and the feet are the lowest, considered dirty and unfit. That's why people always take their shoes off when entering a house, and why it's a mark of reverence to bow down and touch a treasured elder's feet.

It's also why a place like the Taj Mahal has such significance. There's a spiritual reverance there. When Nicole and I made it to the monument, it was a surreal site, a mausoleum of white marble shooting out of the earth, surrounded by plush, long gardens. It was elegant. And emotional. Everything it was created to be.

The story goes that, in 1631, Shah Jahan, who was emperor during the most prosperous period of the Mughal empire, was desolate and heartbroken when his third wife, Mumtaz Mahal, died during childbirth. Gauhara Begum was their fourteenth child. He began construction of the Taj Mahal in 1632 as an ode to his love. Since no architect in the kingdom was capable of conceiving such a project, he summoned the most renowned Persian architect. Then he killed the latter's fiancée, so that together they could share the same terrible grief. In Emperor Shah Jahan's words, this is the Taj Mahal:

> Should guilty seek asylum here,
> Like one pardoned, he becomes free from sin.
> Should a sinner make his way to this mansion,
> All his past sins are to be washed away.
> The sight of this mansion creates sorrowing sighs;
> And the sun and the moon shed tears from their eyes.
> In this world this edifice has been made;
> To display thereby the creator's glory.

After we left the Taj Mahal, the accident happened. And in a way, I think Nicole and I had expected it the whole time. The driving there is so chaotic, the people so restless and quick that they don't worry about swiping by within an eyelash of you. It happened many times, but finally it came too close. A car cut in after abruptly passing a truck and hit me square on. I felt the cracking in my entire body. I flew through the air and landed on the burning asphalt, skidding across the pavement. There were deep skin abrasions, bruises, contusions, and a hairline fracture of the elbow. Even to this day, I feel it sometimes.

But, the worst part of the accident wasn't the pain; it was the people's reaction. The truck drove on, and the car did too, with only one person in the vehicle even bothering to turn around and look. And then within seconds, it was a beehive all around us. People were clustered close. But they didn't want to help. They were pointing and laughing.

Nicole did the best she could to shelter me and disinfect my wounds, and then we both got on the motorcycle and sped away, trying to find a spare plot of peace in that chaotic country of wide eyes and close faces.

Three days later, we returned to the spot to make up the miles. I couldn't skip out on the truth of our journey because of a little pain and anger. If we learned one thing in India, it was that it's an elastic place. It will not easily suit your plans, but it will change them a million times. It's the kind of place fraught with difficulty and marvel, so thick with indecision that you must learn to bend with it or be bent by it.

When people ask me now about running India, I tell them running India is impossible except for the ultra-persistent person who is absolutely willing to risk everything—even death on the road. Nicole and I were extremely fortunate. Despite Nicole's seizures amongst the throngs of humanity crowding around her and my being hit by a vehicle, we both survived. It was love of adventure, love of nature, love for each other, and love for the kids and those in extreme poverty that helped us survive.

By the time we left, we had 14,538 kilometers (9,033 miles) under our belt and a new sense of resolve and appreciation.

CHAPTER TWENTY-FOUR

The Only Decent Man in the Land

"Gratitude is the beginning of civility, of decency and goodness, of a recognition that we cannot afford to be arrogant. We should walk with the knowledge that we will need help every step of the way."
—Gordon B. Hinckley

It was with a mix of delight and trepidation that we returned to South America—the place that had held us in its hand so long during the American Challenge. For our first stop, we found ourselves in Santiago again, a city where we had our layover in 1994 on the way to Ushuaia.

Santiago is one of those cities nestled in the palm of mountains. The snowcapped Andeans to the east, followed by a small pool of coastal peaks to the west. If the day is clear, the view is stunning. But most days in Santiago aren't clear; they're afflicted by smog and noise. The splendor is buried in dirt.

But, thankfully, when we arrived in Santiago the second time, all was clear. An omen of a beautiful road ahead. Nicole sat in a chair at the airport, waiting for our luggage. Bags hung under her eyes, clearly tired from the flying, traveling, and, of course, the road. But opposite her sat a little girl with gorgeous blonde hair like Goldilocks, who was blind to fatigue and saw only loveliness.

"Look, Papa!" the little girl cried. "The lady has painted eyes; how pretty that is. Papa, look, her eyes have the same color as the world!"

The child was thrilled and wandered up to Nicole, only slightly hesitant, and handed her a piece of chocolate.

And, just like that, Nicole was revived.

In Santiago, life was ablaze. Everything was a spectacle. Everything was as bright and friendly as the child. A big top in a circus, everything an uproar. Commotion of the most colorful form. Music sprouted from street corners. People danced in the Plaza de Armas, garnished in elegance and liveliness. It is the kind of city where modernity and history join forces, culminating in exquisiteness.

We spent only two weeks in Chile before moving onto Argentina—the country of wind, tangos, and steak. Stretching across the bulk of southern South America, Argentina takes up nearly the same landmass as India, but with less than 4% of India's population.

By then, the weather was turning cold at night and, when we could afford it, we'd look for a cheap, run-down hotel that could at least provide a few walls and a roof. One particularly cold night while I was looking for a place to sleep in a village in the shadow of the mountains, Nicole approached an old gentleman. He had an old face, tired and worn by years of work. He was sweeping the street, stirring up dust and intrigue.

"Everyone here is mean," he said in passing, talking as if to the air.

Nicole looked at him, prodding him on. "And you, are you also mean?"

He shook his head furiously, the sparse gray strands of hair swiping his forehead.

"Absolutely not. I am the only decent man in the land."

Nicole laughed at this and handed him a cap, a gift to make him feel more comfortable. His eyes went bright with excitement, and he tucked the cap under his arm quickly, hiding it away like the prized possession it was. He promised he would wear it on Sunday, the Lord's Day.

And then, like a stray thought, he looked past her, noticing for the first time how she had made it into town.

"You have a funny motorcycle," he said, eyeing our trailer.

Nicole tried to explain it was our home, that we were running the world, but the response didn't satisfy the old fellow. To him, what we were doing didn't make any sense. He was certain she was transporting some contraband inside. Or perhaps a TV or radio. He shuffled his way over to our trailer and poked about, fascinated.

As he lingered there, a girl passed by with a rather lovely face.

"Did you notice how pretty she was?" Nicole asked, trying to goad him away from the motorcycle and onto another subject.

The sly, old man, though, didn't take the bait, "What do you mean? The Cordillera de los Andes?"

And he looked up at the mountain peaks, giving them the slightest wink.

But, the old man was right—the Andes Mountains were just as beautiful as they were daunting. The nature of Argentina was certainly as captivating as its people.

Nicole and I would learn that intimately three days later when we left the city to run the mountains ourselves. It was an unreasonably hard journey, but a necessary one to keep moving forward. To pull oneself up to the heights of the cordillera is a remarkable feat, but to go back down isn't any easier—especially for the runner. My knees were pushed and bent and given weight they never desired.

By the time we'd made it up the side of the mountain to the pass, we were dog-tired, but feeling invigorated. The Argentinean mountains have character. Though steep, they are boastful, proud, and dominating. Nicole and I felt at home among them. There was something about their power that reminded us of the Alps.

The invigoration stopped, though, at the peak. Just when we thought we were on the downhill side, a voice shouted out to us: "Stop! You can't pass!"

Out of nowhere, we'd come upon a military post. A handful of guards looked at us, crossing their arms and looking at our trailer and bike in a curious, but dismayed fashion. We knew we were in a jam. We had come so far, but we were entirely at their mercy. If they didn't let us pass, we'd have to go all the way down and find a way around. I tried to explain our situation as politely as possible, but they didn't want to budge. The road, they said, wasn't made for running. We must turn around.

The old man had been right after all. There was a mean streak in the Argentine blood!

Nicole moved off to the side, fuming, but I didn't want to give up. We hadn't turned around on the tour yet, and I certainly didn't want to start then.

"Look," I said. "If we cannot pass, I must have a written document, because we have to render an account to the president of our country… it will be really embarrassing for the public image of Argentina, because this will be the first country in four years that would prevent us from continuing our route as planned."

It was a bluff, of course, but I had to pray it would work. We simply could not begin again.

The military leader told us to wait and he went off to the side, speaking with his cohorts for no less than two hours to come to a decision. Finally, his impromptu huddle came to a finish.

"You may pass," he said, "But be careful. You never know what's out there." And with that knowing threat, he opened up the barrier.

We finally reached Mendoza, the end point of the first major leg of the journey and, more importantly, a city very close to the mythical Cerro Aconcagua, the highest spot in the Americas. I am a mountain guide at heart. I will always be, and so the Aconcagua tempted me. Even though we'd already run 31,000 kilometers (19,263 miles), I knew I could not deny the call of the mountains, and so in February of 2004, we briefly paused our journey so I could summit.

I left the base camp of Aconcagua by the normal way (Plaza de Mulas, 4,300 meters) at six o'clock in the morning. I arrived at the summit after seven hours and fifteen minutes of climbing, passing by these high-altitude camps: Camp Canada, Nido de Condores, Berlin, Independencia, and then ending with La Traversia and La Canaleta.

While filming with my little camera, I recorded my first impressions on the summit. Too much emotion…. I thanked Nicole. I realized that I had carried a little of the heart of my daughter, Clara, and of my son, Steve, in my light backpack. I thought of Mama, to whom I owe my love of the mountains, of my brother Yves, also a mountain guide, of Gilbert, of Ron, of Susan, and of so many other friends.

And then, before being frozen by the effects of a temperature of minus-35°C—equal to minus-31°F—and a fearsome wind, I went all the way back down to the base camp in one stretch. It's a stretch totally unlike the others—a marathon for which the main difficulty resided in the constant search for oxygen.

Aconcagua—the highest mountain in the world after those of the Himalayan chain—was conquered for the first time by a guide from Valais (my home canton) in 1897. I was overcome with a sense of belonging.

When I returned back to Mendoza, Nicole looked restored. Acclimated even. While I had been gone, returning to my mountain life, she too had been returning to a sense of normalcy. Sleeping in sheets. Waking up and seeing the same people, day after day. It's amazing how little details like that can make such a difference. For Nicole, Mendoza will remain a little haven of peace on this long road of the world. And for me, it will always stand as a powerful juncture: the point of departure and the point of return for another great adventure, and another dream realized.

CHAPTER TWENTY-FIVE

Running Through Hurricanes

"*There are some things you learn best in calm, and some in storm.*"
—**Willa Cather**

There's an indiscernible border that runs through the Eastern United States. It's unmarked, but, without a doubt, you know when you've crossed it. It's the line dividing the north and the south—the cool and steely from the warm and spacious. If you've ever been there, you know people are region loyal in the States—particularly those from a south that's so deep, it's no longer the south at all; it's Florida.

Living in a state that stretches to the southern tip of the U.S., Floridians are in a world of their own. Miami, the Everglades, and the Keys all cluster together in a humid mix of swamps, alligators, tropical storms, orange groves, luscious palm trees, and biting mosquitoes. It's an eco-system of unparalleled beauty and mystery, where the people are as colorful and sultry as their surroundings.

Nicole and I arrived in the States through Miami. Our motorcycle got lost en route from Rio and ended up accidently being sent to New York, where it circled around the Statue of Liberty a few times before it made its way back down to the right harbor. This, naturally, meant a good long wait. And while our life sat there on pause and we sweated away in the damp heat, we met Charley.

Nicole went out to the pharmacy one afternoon to run some basic errands and heard, out of the corner of her ear, a conversation between an elderly woman and a pharmacist that bothered her.

"We'll have to get reserves of water and food," the old lady said. "It'll be any time now, I hear."

Her expression was remarkably calm, but Nicole found their conversation startling. What could they mean? Reserves? Why reserves? And *what* would be any time now? Trying as best she could to decipher their English and communicate, Nicole asked what was going on. The two women with their deep Floridian tans and southern tongues tried to explain to Nicole—who spoke little English—that a hurricane was on its way. It was predicted to be the most devastating storm to Florida's coast in over a decade.

Nicole thanked the ladies and hurried back to the hotel and asked at the reception desk whether they had heard about this, too. Was it true?

"This evening," the receptionist told her, "you'll need to stay in your room and not come out for twenty-four hours. Simply wait until it passes."

By the time Nicole got back to the room, she was in a panic. Her first impulse was to fill up the bathtub with water, to unplug everything electrical, and to buy drinking water. Her head was already filled with all the people who were going to lose so much, even their lives. We turned on the television set. All the normal programming was interrupted. Without a break, information shot across the screen, posting pictures and data on the brewing Hurricane Charley. One of the journalists finished his report with the less than encouraging words: "We wish you the best, but we fear the worst. Good luck!"

That night, we tried to sleep as best we could, but toward one o'clock in the morning, the storm was raging. It was incredibly violent, something like the end of the world. Through the window, we witnessed a spectacle. Trees snapped, roofs flew into the sky, bridges collapsed, and cars were flipped over like leaves.

We looked at the ceiling, hoping it would hold. The windows seemed to be withstanding the storm, but how long could they possibly last? And afterward, what would happen? For an entire day, we lived in anguish, but then, thank goodness, Charley began to calm down.

As it turned out, August 2004 was one of the most active months for storms in decades. There were seven major hurricanes, of which Charley was the most catastrophic. It had started off as a modest storm system in the Western Atlantic, and it didn't really become anything threatening until it reached the coast of Cuba, churning winds up to 105 miles per hour. As it crossed the island, it picked up steam and pummeled into Florida, taking twenty-five lives and causing over 7.5 billion in damage. In total, Charley lasted from August 9 to August 15, and, at its peak intensity, had 150 mph (240 km/h) winds.

After a few days, as Charley finally cleared, we got our motorcycle back and could start running again. With only 5,000 kilometers left to go (3,107 miles), we knew we were near the end. But the storm had exhausted us, and the heat was oppressive. Every mile or two, I had to stop and drink something, sponge off my face, and regain composure. In sweltering Florida, where my head felt like a cauliflower in a large pressure cooker, I couldn't run more than nineteen miles a day. And Charley wasn't the only hurricane that we encountered; we actually ran through pouring rain on the fringes of three different hurricanes, as we continued up the East Coast.

But when doubt overcomes you, you must chase it away, blow it in another direction. So every morning we set out again, one more day, and then yet another . . . 35,281 kilometers [21,923 miles] and counting.

CHAPTER TWENTY-SIX

Losing Nora

"No language can express the power, and beauty, and heroism, and majesty of a mother's love. It shrinks not where man cowers, and grows stronger where man faints, and over wastes of worldly fortunes sends the radiance of its quenchless fidelity like a star."

—Edwin Hubbell Chapin

I don't know if I can explain it, really, but from the moment that day started out, Nicole and I were pretty listless. Most days we could summon the motivation to get on the road, but some days, like this one, it just felt like there was an invisible stumbling block.

It was November of 2004. We were on the east coast of the United States, heading up to New York. It was a nice fall, not too cold, and we'd be home in no less than five months.

A woman was standing on the side of the road at a red light. She began speaking to us in French, which made us curious. You didn't hear that often in the States. "Are you believers?" she asked. Nicole and I didn't really know how to respond. The light turned green and we went up a few hundred meters, but she followed us, shoving a brochure in Nicole's face with the title: "When Death Strikes a Loved One."

Normally, we would have thrown something like that in the trash.

But, for no apparent reason, Nicole kept it, putting it into the trailer. I shrugged it off.

I ran thirty-six kilometers (twenty-two miles) that day, and they were hard-fought ones—that's for certain. By the time we set up camp that evening, I was entirely exhausted.

Nicole fingered the brochure in her hands. I could tell her mind was reeling. She'd always get this look on her face when she was really thinking about something.

"Serge?" she asked. "How would you react if you lost someone close to you? Like me? Or your mom? Or one of your children?"

It's funny how little we actually talked about death, given how close it was to us all time. But that's probably because I didn't think it worthwhile to give too much room to the idea.

In my head, I'll be on the move until I'm a hundred years old and, after that, I'll take my chair and stay quiet for the rest.

I have always said I'll need a minimum of five lives to live half of my dreams and a sixth one to stay quiet. I'm not scared to die, but I'm in no hurry.

And so, I imagine, I hope the same things for the people I love, and so I think only about their life and their potential, not how I could lose them.

But sitting there, thinking about loss, I imagined I knew how I would feel.

"Probably like everyone else."

We stopped talking about it then. Frankly, I wasn't in the mood. When you've had a hard day, you want to be buoyed up. You don't want to dwell on all the potential bad things that could happen. So Nicole got up to go take a shower at the campsite, and I sat there reading.

The phone rang then. A very distinct, piercing sound. We always had our satellite phone with us just in case. But we rarely used it.

My brother Yves was on the line.

"Hello!" I said. It was so good to hear from someone at home. Whenever the days felt a little long, a familiar voice was as restorative as a full night's sleep.

But my brother's voice was not as excited as mine was.

"You need to sit down, Serge," he said, not beating around the issue.

When Nicole came back from the shower, she found me entirely pale. I could hardly breathe. I could hardly sit up. The grief was so pungent, I didn't imagine I could really do anything. I told Nicole to lie down. And in some part of her, I think she already knew what had happened.

"Mama Nora has left us," I said.

She had passed away in her home, two days short of her seventy-fifth birthday, in the same kitchen where my dad had died of a heart attack many years before.

When I left Sion, I imagined the worst things would follow us. *We* would have to be prepared for what *we* met on the road—the danger, the disease, the potential of losing one another. But I hadn't given a thought really to what could be happening back in Switzerland. I just imagined their lives would go on as usual, and we'd return to the same full, smiling faces that we had left, eager to sweep us up in their arms and kiss us on the cheeks. What trouble could there be in Sion? Peaceful, sweet Sion.

But my mother, always known for her long walks and ventures, had gone on her last stroll, one she wouldn't return from. And while I was running up the east coast, headed to the bright lights of New York, she was headed to another set of lights, thousands and thousands of kilometers away.

I didn't understand it. The pain was like nothing else I had ever felt. Worse than any physical strain I'd encountered. My breath was heavy, quick, and then it would disappear and I couldn't breathe at all. It didn't make sense to me, and the ridiculousness of it all was painful.

She was in great shape. Just three years prior, she had again climbed the 4,027-meter peak named Allalin with my brother, Yves, as her guide. Nicole always affectionately called her "the little goat of the mountains." Who could do that and then just disappear? She had boundless energy. She had brought me my love of nature, my kinship with the mountains, and my passion for the extreme. She was one of the main reasons I was able to do what I was doing; I could not have run around the world without her.

And yet, my mother took her leave as she had lived. Quietly, peacefully, disturbing no one.

I needed to go home. But how? Finally, I thought of my distant American relative in Kansas City. I first met him in California while running the American Challenge. Joe had become like a brother to me. I hurriedly dialed his number, but when he answered, I was just rambling. To make understanding even worse, he was in the middle of the lobby hubbub of a large hotel and couldn't comprehend what I was saying. At first, he thought that Nicole had died. Finally, I was able to convey the thought that my mother had died. In brotherly fashion, he told me not to worry, that he would make all the arrangements for our flight to Geneva and purchase the tickets.

Nicole had lost her grandmother, Luisa, during the American Challenge and her beloved Aunt Arlette just a few months prior, while we were running North Carolina, so she understood my pain firsthand and comforted me as much as she could, but she was grief-stricken, too. She'd grown to love my mother dearly. I wanted to get back home as quickly as possible. I was desperate to see my mom, to have the chance to say some sort of goodbye.

Thankfully, Joe got us on a flight the very next day. We had just spent the previous weekend with him and his lovely wife, Judy, in Kansas City, and then accompanied them to a Roetheli family reunion.

When we got back to Sion, I spent many hours at my mother's side. I talked to her at length, telling her the stories of my time on the World Tour. Somewhere I knew she could hear me and that she'd be happy knowing what we'd done. I also knew that she would tell us that no matter what happened, we had to persevere. We had to keep going. I could almost hear her scolding me like I was once again a little boy. "Serge, it's part of life. People pass away. This is the price you pay for loving someone. You will hurt. It is natural. But you will heal. Remember: You are only five months short of your goal. You must keep going! Life always continues."

And that it does. So, in a few days time, Nicole and I boarded the plane again. When we landed, we were at the gates of New York. And, while still shaky with grief, we were certain my mother was at our sides as we made our entrance into the great Manhattan.

CHAPTER TWENTY-SEVEN

The Swiss Forrest Gump

"One belongs to New York instantly, one belongs to it as much in five minutes as in five years."

—Tom Wolfe

It was the early hours when we took our first steps out onto the Brooklyn Bridge—one of the oldest suspension bridges in the United States. Built in 1883, the bridge connects New York's famed boroughs of Manhattan and Brooklyn, straddling the East River. It's iconic to say the least.

It was a picturesque November morning in New York. Clouds were sparse, and light was streaming onto the pre-dawn darkness from the freshly-opened restaurants and office buildings. Vendors were setting up on street corners, and newspaper boys were hoisting black and white papers in their hands, like it was a throwback to a time when print ruled the world.

I was excited that morning. That day we were going to cover twenty miles, heading over the bridge, down the avenue, and ending at the site of the World Trade Center. Out of all the stretches on the tour, this was the one I'd been looking forward to the most. Running down the infamous Fifth Avenue—miles of uninterrupted American bliss, the most expensive road in the world.

Fifth Avenue starts at Washington Square Park in Greenwich Village and heads north toward the heart of Midtown, cresting Central Park, creating the boundary between the Upper East Side and Harlem.

It's pretty hard to explain the emotion we felt arriving on Fifth Avenue. For as long as I'd been looking forward to it, Nicole had been dreading it. The immensity of New York overwhelmed her. It was one clogged artery after another. How were we doing to run through it? Drive through it? But as we steadily moved in, I could see her relaxing. New York has that effect on people. It can grow on you instantaneously.

Some days, running didn't feel like a task. It didn't feel like something I'd been doing for days and months and years. The simplest thing—like a place—can make an old-hat action feel very new and fresh. And New York was just the kind of place that could have that power.

Nicole said later that New York is the city of all superlatives: astonishing, unnerving, fascinating, so many adjectives that seem to fit it to a tee. Internationality explodes here. More than half the population comes from somewhere else. It's as though a mania for greatness prevailed here: the highest, the most beautiful, the biggest. The architectural feats are phenomenal. New York also wears a cloak of multicolored lights. We've been everywhere, and I can tell you, no other city has this effect.

The sun was cresting in the sky by the time we got to the other side of the bridge and onto Fifth Avenue. The display windows were richly decorated; even though it was morning, lights sparkled everywhere. You could tell Christmas was near. The five lanes of traffic stretching across the avenue were already busy, starting to cluster with cabs and delivery trucks, all heading north. New York was being predictable, and so were its people. With every corner we turned, they were there to meet us with stares.

We received a lot of curious looks around the world. In India, people stare at you closely. They get within inches of your face and pry their eyes wide open – but with wonder and curiosity. Not with condescension or hatred or scorn. In Europe people look at you out of the corner of their eyes, catching hushed glimpses when they think you can't see them. But, New Yorkers aren't quiet ones. The city and its inhabitants never balk from an opportunity to tell you exactly what they think.

A driver in his yellow-checkered cab, stuck at a red light at the foot of the bridge, flagged us down. He took one look at me in my short shorts and Nicole on her motorcycle, with the trailer rumbling loyally behind her, and he said the first thing that came to his mind. "What the hell are you two doing?"

He was a heavyset guy, a little round on the tummy, with an un-shaven beard and a cup of Dunkin Donuts coffee in a cup holder. His cell phone sat in the adjacent cup holder, and he was thumping a news-paper on the passenger's seat, as though he were banging out a tune to pass the time. His voice had been curt, but it was also a little curious. Kind even, when you got down to it.

"We certainly get our lot of interesting individuals around here, but I don't think I've ever seen anybody quite like you two."

This was saying something, of course. The city isn't typically a place where you stand out. You'll see a man in a pressed Brooks Brothers suit standing on a corner, talking on his phone, while two feet away, shaking a change cup, is a man wearing bread wrappers on his feet for shoes. And then two feet away from them is a woman dressed, head to toe, in Barbie doll pink, her hair spiked stiff in bright rays of fuchsia.

To catch attention in New York is more than unusual; it's a miracle.

Nicole pulled the motorcycle over, and we indulged him. We told him where we had started, how long we'd been going, and what we were trying to do. His eyes were a bit buggy. And every sentence or two, he'd slap the steering wheel and sputter, "You're kidding me, right?"

By the time I was through talking, the man was downright flab-bergasted.

"Well, I'll be damned," he said, and he honked his horn loudly. And then, once again for emphasis. And then he got on his radio in the car and started churning it out on the New York cab airwaves.

"Guys, you'll never believe this," he said. "I got the freakin' Swiss Forrest Gump over here." And then he repeated the exact story I had told him. Though perhaps with a few more expletives.

He honked his horn energetically as we ran away, throwing his arm out the window and pumping it in the air.

I had a rush in my stride as we moved forward out onto the avenue.

Meeting people on the road who support you in your dreams is a kind of lifeblood. Their good words and hearty smiles are as nourishing as any home-cooked meal. But I had no idea how contagious his enthusiasm would be.

If you've ever seen New York light up at Christmas, you might have an idea of what happens when an idea floods and overtakes the city. How one spark can ignite a fire that rampages avenue after avenue, overwhelming lampposts and windowpanes, parks and storefronts. New York is a contagious city with a loyalty so fierce and so fluent, even little ladies in the Paris bistros with their tiny lap dogs know about it.

And that day, the cabbies caught hold of something they were excited about. Something, I imagine, that reminded them of what New York is all about and why they came there in the first place. The city is a magical place. It's where the impossible doesn't exist. And for that stretch of time, running down the Avenue, to them I was a New Yorker, conquering the most unlikely feat. Proving everyone wrong.

The horns overtook Fifth Avenue. They rang reliably and energetically with the occasional cabbie sticking his head out the window, "Way to go, Serge! Run, Serge, run!"

It was a brief moment of notoriety, where hundreds of people finally understood what we were doing and why we were doing it. And there's probably not a whole lot in this world that feels better than being known.

Pedestrians, businessmen, and street vendors looked around, wondering what had gotten into the city's water that day. They looked at the cabbies as though they were all drunk, and then went on their way as though that might, in fact, be a normal thing.

It was our little secret. Our secret with the greatest city's entire cab service. A secret of bells and triumphs and running down Fifth Avenue all the way to the finish of our dreams.

But then, in the midst of it all, I stopped. We had passed our 37,000th kilometer (22,990 miles) right there on Fifth Avenue. The number might seem insignificant or random to most, but it meant we'd put another thousand kilometers under our belt, complete with unforgettable encounters, moments of restlessness, and pockets of pure bliss. It also meant we were getting closer to Switzerland. Only 3,500 kilometers left (2,175 miles) to run. There were still some months to go, but in comparison to the whole journey, I felt as though I could reach out and touch it.

Continuing our ritual for each thousand kilometers completed, I kissed Nicole to mark the 37,000th kilometer passed and then started running again. Not thirty minutes later, we'd finished our leg of the journey for the day, right in front of where the Twin Towers of the World Trade Center used to stand. A welcoming committee of friends waited for us there—our Swiss friend, Henri Rappaz, a cameraman, and his son Dorian, Ron and Susan Zamber, who had come directly from Alaska, and our dear relative from Kansas City, Joe Roetheli, who had been following us closely and supporting us as we'd traveled the world's streets and roads.

In a place so far away, it felt as though we were coming home.

CHAPTER TWENTY-EIGHT

Catch Your Stride

"Travel is fatal to prejudice, bigotry, and narrow-mindedness, and many of our people need it sorely on these accounts. Broad, wholesome, charitable views of men and things cannot be acquired by vegetating in one little corner of the earth all one's lifetime."

—Mark Twain

Is it any surprise that running feels so natural? More than a million people run marathons every year. They lace up their shoes, pin on their numbers, and trek out onto the pavement to boil out the 26.2 miles because something in their mind, body, and soul just feels right when it's striding and free. Even when it's bleeding, cut, twinging in pain, or cramping, the body is free and it is trying. And inevitably—if you keep going—you will always catch your stride.

There are many animals that are excellent runners. They're shaped individually for swiftness. But humans are built for endurance. Harvard anthropology professor Daniel Lieberman said, "Humans are terrible athletes in terms of power and speed, but we're phenomenal at slow and steady. We're the tortoises of the animal kingdom."

I don't mind being the tortoise, though—to take the whole experience in with persistence and might. To see something all the way through rather than to give out in a bright, mad burst. In a way, we humans are suited for the big picture rather than the little one. The rule is simple and unchanging: always keep going.

By the time we hit Switzerland, I could feel it in every part of my legs. They knew the trek was coming to an end. One stride after another sprang forward, and I was aware of the pavement bouncing off my toes, if perhaps only with slightly less enthusiasm than they had nearly five years ago. Each of my legs had by now plunged me forward over thirty-three million strides on this journey. But I was still moving forward, the springy tendons in my legs functioning like large rubber bands, stockpiling energy and then releasing it so I could bite off portions of the pavement. I should have been tired of running by then; I should have hated it even. But eighteen miles under the belt that last day and there was no heaving, no great exasperation. My arms moved backward and forward, compensating for each other with each swing.

No, I would not say I was tired. The only thing I felt that day was able.

We turned a bend in the road and I saw what was the first glimpse of our hometown on the horizon. It's such a strange feeling to return when all you've done for half a decade is go. You'd think I'd be relieved. And in a way I was. Whenever you leave a place, you are giving something up. People, memories, comfort, a sense of abiding security. Home is the warm blanket, the timber in the fire, the foundation that makes everything new and insecure grab a firm hold and grow. I love where I am from. And its reassuring silhouette reminded me that Nicole and I belonged somewhere. We no longer had to live out of an overnight bag, plunking down tents and rapping on doors for meals. We no longer had to beg or be in need. We could hang up pictures and sleep in fresh, clean sheets. We, in a word, belonged.

Would it be possible to hide the pride I had running toward that corner of the world we were privileged to call home, watching the Matterhorn with its chiseled peak flexing in the sky? In Switzerland, I knew what to expect—the Aletsch Glacier, the longest in all of Europe. The railway lines that claw up the mountainside. The submerging contentment of the hot springs. The magic of the small towns and the people who inhabit them—those who are not distracted by the rapid success of the world, but who are enthralled by the success that has existed for years upon years in the valleys and on the mountains. I had seen too many people on this trip who were skimping by, hand to mouth, dwelling in shortage. Clothes worn down to bare threads, the fibers caked in mud. Houses built of scrap metal, cardboard, and wood. Piecemeal poverty and war dots the world like dandelions. It would be selfish not to feel blessed.

All the same, though, just as much as Switzerland is my home, in a way, the road had become just as familiar and comforting. The strangeness had become reassuring. And I had to wonder what life would be like waking up in the same bed—my bed—two days in a row. What would it be like not to push my mind and body to such a degree that it writhed not only in pain, but in satisfaction? How would I exist without the road? To leave this behind felt—in some parts of my heart—uncertain and wrong. Strange even. For me, running is second nature, as everyday as getting a cup of coffee, checking the mail, turning down the covers.

I looked straight ahead, the mountains jutting like sandcastles straight into the sky. I could hear my feet treading, left after right. A built-in metronome, they were the dedicated clockwork that kept me going. Sometimes when I think about it, I can't believe all the places they've taken me. Through the Sahara, darting along the Great Ocean Road, sifting through the bustle of Times Square. Cape Town. Sydney. Portugal. Argentina. I have smelled, touched, seen, and heard the world wake up, witnessing the sun peel into a new sky each day, transcending time zones, languages, and customs. Running can take you anywhere. Running is, in a word, universal.

Leonardo da Vinci wrote that feet were "a masterpiece of engineering and a work of art." And the man was right. It's a madhouse down there—each foot is constructed of twenty-eight bones, which is equal to one fourth of all the bones present in the human body. Not to mention the 107 ligaments, thirty joints, and nineteen muscles. And all of those separate, unique pieces work together to move us forward, creating an unthinkably efficient, powerful, and strong composition. Our feet are our own integrated locomotives.

More than that, though, no two feet in the world have the same blueprint—not even your own. And they're always altering, adapting to your height and weight, whether you're standing or sitting, moving or pausing. Our feet are intuitive. They understand us. They want to help us get from point A to point B—whatever we decide those points might be, whether it's a block away or worlds apart.

As we neared our last few miles, I peered over my shoulder to see Nicole at my side. Pride wishes to say I could have done this alone. A part of every human succumbs to that conceit, believing self-reliance can take you as far as collaboration. But autonomy is poor company for solidarity. I could not have done this without Nicole. Not one country, much less one continent. Her pace was steady, a timid but sure smile pressed on her face. I had never seen so much earnestness in a pair of eyes, her green irises glinting, catching flecks of sun as she slowly paced beside me.

Love is a curious thing. When you meet someone for the first time and you tumble into these feelings that make your head ache and your heart pound and your bed restless, you see all the flawless things about them. The thousand-watt smile. The way their hair perfectly frames their face. The laugh that catches on your ears. And you play those perfect moments in your mind over and over again. Panoramas of everything you've always dreamed of. But those things are tumbleweeds. They come and they go. Real love is caught up in the moments that you won't frame on the mantel and set out at dinner parties. It's full of unshaved legs and a lack of showers. A pale face, untouched by makeup. It's caring for someone as they vomit, and reel, and shout hysterics, succumbing to cerebral malaria. It's running miles in the pouring rain or the parched, empty desert. It's standing in the thick of frustration and desperation, thirst and fatigue. Love is being intimate with the worst and choosing to stay. Love is a choice, not a given. And I would not have chosen to go through the potholes with anyone else.

People might gawk at the feats of the Lance Armstrongs of the world. And there's reason to, of course. But, like most modern-day endurance athletes, he hasn't once mounted a bike or launched a feat without the diligent, watchful eye of his team who constantly screens, assists, and pampers. His training, schedule, and eating regimen are tackled with an uncanny precision. A Band-Aid always in wait for the most freshly-developed paper cut. He has sponsors, physical therapy, the most advanced equipment, and techniques.

While I... well, I had Nicole. The beautiful, strong, courageous Nicole who rode beside me patiently, who could massage my feet to health, and who could scold me into persistence. She carried me in a way no amount of modern technology or knowledge ever could.

When I felt as though I should be wasted, as though my feet could not possibly carry me another inch, she recharged me. She got me back onto the road and surged me forward with all the simplicity and ease of a raging current.

It should be no surprise to me that two of the most natural human instincts—love and running—have propelled me through these six continents, these 25,000 very long miles. That they have intertwined to make the impossible possible. But if I have learned anything from these five years on the road, it is that while the world can be remarkably small, it is always infinitely vast in its miracles and beauty.

The hum of Nicole's motorcycle faded slightly as the town came into focus. There was a mass of people in front of us, cloaked in happiness. Banners were hanging from buildings and trickling from the fingers of jumping children. Balloons buoyed in the air, spiriting our welcome. I could make out the faces of family and friends, my daughter and son. But I looked over my shoulder one last time—out to a vast stretch of road that was void of any car or human. Not so much as a rustle of dust flecked the vision. And I knew without a doubt that this would not be my last adventure.

We pulled into the throng of celebrations. Nicole and I were both weeping. And for the last time in five years, I heard her click off the motor.

EPILOGUE

"There is a great deal of unmapped country within us."

—George Eliot

As I sit here writing this, it has now been seven years since the World Tour came to an end, and I can say to you from the other side of the finish line: Everything is possible. Nothing is impossible.

It seemed quite the extraordinary notion that I could set off and run the circumference of the world, over 25,000 miles. Whenever you start something and you think about the whole picture, it's overwhelming. But when you take it mile by mile, or when you just look at the day's tasks and not the year's toils, impossible has a way of crawling out of your vocabulary rather quickly.

In *Bird by Bird*, Anne Lamott quotes the wisdom of E.L. Doctorow. It's like driving a car at night. You can see only as far as your headlights, but you can make the whole trip that way. You don't have to see where you're going, you don't have to see your destination or everything you will pass along the way. You just have to see two or three feet ahead of you."

And that's exactly how I ran the World Tour—just a few feet at a time.

I was perhaps not the first to accomplish this feat, but it doesn't do you much good to be the kind of person who gets caught up in records and recognition. Isn't the most important thing, after all, that you do what you say you're going to do as well as you can?

The principle my mother taught me will never let you down: Let your yes be yes, and your no be no.

As to what we're now doing, Nicole is working in a long-term care hospital in Sion, which is quite consistent with her concern for the less fortunate.

I am now back in my beloved mountains, working again as a mountain guide. I wake up every day and see the snow-crested peaks from my window. And while I've returned back to my true home in the Alps, many things have changed.

I am no longer with Nicole. This fact always shocks people to a degree and saddens them, especially those who know and understand our journey. People wonder how a couple that has been through so much can fall out of love. They think the World Tour tore us apart. But in the end, they're looking at it the wrong way. It is quite the opposite. The World Tour is what held us together for so long. We were bonded by a journey, by a hope and a style of life, and when that road came to an end, we gradually realized that ours had, too.

We still respect each other. There is no hatred. Just an understanding that you have to follow wherever the road leads, and it might not take you where you had planned to go. There is a price to pay for your dreams, and sometimes that price is saying goodbye.

We have both moved on to new loves and new adventures, and I look back on our eighteen years of marriage with a distinct feeling of thankfulness and pride. I am astounded by the woman Nicole was in the midst of the desert, in the throngs of Bangladesh, in the icy cold of the Alaskan winter. She has always been so strong and so powerful. I'm not certain anyone else could have done what she did. For me, our separation will never take away from the story, which is one of love, of freedom, of kids, and of grand exploration. And I know we will always maintain an important friendship.

I have not stopped adventuring. Just a year ago, I spent 63 days in a twenty-two-foot by five-foot canoe, paddling across the Atlantic Ocean—from the Canary Islands to Barbados—with my friend Ole

Elmer of Vancouver, BC. And, each week I am on the mountainside, facing a new challenge on nature's great face. And tomorrow? Well, we shall see.

I know this book is inadequate in so many ways. If it takes five years to run the world, how many pages could it possibly take to explain its adventures? No matter how long I kept going, I could not do it justice. But I hope somewhere in these pages you've found truth. And more than that, I hope you've found the confidence to pursue your dreams. Let your yes be yes and your no be no, then take it one step at a time and no more. Remember: everything is possible, nothing is impossible.

As for me, I will keep on the move until I am a hundred years old, and after that I will take a chair and stay quiet for the rest.

The journey awaits....

—Serge

AFTERWORD

Over the past year and a half, we have served as the creative team that worked in conjunction with The Roetheli Lil' Red Foundation representatives to produce the inspirational documentary film and companion book entitled *The 25,000 Mile Love Story*. As the film's producers, scriptwriter, marketer, and publisher, we've been blessed to witness unique insights into the life of Serge Roetheli—a man of incredible endurance achievements who has gone through life, success after success, largely unknown.

A man of many accolades, Serge has done everything from running the distance of the circumference of the world to macheteing his way across the Darien Gap and canoeing across the Atlantic Ocean. These are unthinkable feats standing alone, and frankly it's hard to believe one man could have done so much.

On none of these adventures did Serge go out with large teams or huge corporate sponsors. He didn't have doctors trailing at his feet or nutritionists pumping vitamins down his throat. He simply went out, sometimes with his wife, sometimes with a friend, and willed his way to the finish line with his own persistence, street-smart thinking, passion, determination, and hard work. He wasn't doing it for the accolades or notoriety. He wasn't doing it to beat a record or make an indelible mark. He was doing it because his daily fiber is one that's built from adventure and making a worthwhile journey out of this thing called life.

His wife through the majority of his adventures—the American Challenge and World Tour—was Nicole. And, in her own right, she was a dynamic personality who had the guts to set out on a long, unknown road. How many women do you know who would have left the safety and comfort of their home and friends to risk health issues, injury—and possibly even death—just to ride a motorcycle around the world? We might be so bold as to say we haven't found one yet!

As we've spent these many months learning the details of Serge's adventures, we have become more and more enthralled by the man and his heart. Just as much as his actions, his humility has astounded us. Not unlike the horse, Secretariat, Serge has figuratively been blessed with an extra-large heart—one that allows him to accomplish amazing physical feats, certainly, but that also blesses him with an unparalleled positive, no-quit attitude. There is something uncommonly good beating in the blood of this man that keeps him pushing forward and doing so for the good of others.

There are many people who have completed unbelievable endurance feats in this world. We have studied those heroes and are awed by their stories as well. But—with the breadth and depth of his feats—we can't help but wonder in the back of our minds if the world has been missing the greatest hero? Could Serge Roetheli—the fifty-seven year old man from Switzerland with no team and no doctors—be the greatest endurance athlete of our time?

Below we've listed a few of his many accomplishments so that you, the reader, may get to know the man as we have and then make your own judgment.

Serge, the Runner

As this book details, Serge ran the distance of the circumference of the world. Between February 2000 and May 2005, he ran 25,422 miles in 1,910 days, averaging a marathon every other day for sixty-three months. So far, we've only identified one other person to run the distance of the circumference of the world (Robert Garside), and he completed the feat after numerous false starts and with corporate sponsorship just twenty-six months before Serge did.

As a warm up event for running the world, between January 1995 and December 1997, Serge ran the longest road in the world, The Pan American Highway. He started in Ushuaia/Tierra del Fuego, the southernmost city in the world, and thirty-five months and 14,984 miles later, he ran into Fairbanks, Alaska, in December, with a bone-chilling cold of -24 degrees Fahrenheit, with Nicole at his side on her motorcycle.

Serge has run all or parts of the Sahara Desert (2000), the Atacama Desert (1995), the Sinai Desert (2001), and Death Valley (1986). He also ran from the rim of the Grand Canyon down to the Colorado River and back up the 5,200 feet of ascent in a single day.

Between October, 1989, and May, 1990, Serge ran 4,359 miles in Europe, from Gibralter to Cape North, Norway, mostly in winter. He averaged more than a marathon per day on this entire trip. He also ran Italy from Palermo to Milano, 1,100 miles in forty-one days, averaging just over a marathon per day.

In 1993, Serge also ran more than sixty miles of trail connecting the six Swiss high-altitude mountain cabins with 20,500 feet of ascent and descent in 16 hours and 30 minutes or 3.6 miles per hour up and down mountains.

In 1994, Serge ran a trail of more than eighty miles that connected the five major mountaintops in the Swiss Alps. He did it in just 19 hours and 55 minutes, averaging a speed of four miles per hour.

In 2002 in Nepal, he ran 150 miles through the Himalayan Mountains in just seven days, averaging 0.8 of a marathon per day. Running this Annapurna Circle meant continually going up and down mountains, with the highest point being the Thorong La Pass at 17,589 feet.

Serge, the Climber
In addition to his running, Serge has climbed the highest peaks in Europe, Africa, North America, and South America: Mt. Blanc: 15,782 feet; Mt. Kilimanjaro: 19,341feet; Mt. McKinley: 20,320 feet; and Mt. Aconcagua: 22,841 feet.

Serge has led clients and customers to the peak of Mt. Blanc more than forty times and once solo-climbed the treacherous Peuterey Ridge of Mt. Blanc. He has climbed the Matterhorn (14,690 feet) more than thirty times, and has solo-climbed more than thirty major mountains in the Swiss Alps.

Serge has scaled the 2,600-foot wall of the Lotus Flower Tower in the Northwest Territories of Canada in two days of rock climbing. While in Nepal, in 2002, he and François Germain, a friend and fellow Swiss guide, led an expedition of hikers to the top of 18,470-foot Tent Peak. And, in Ecuador, he led nine customers to the top of five volcanic mountains, including Mt. Chimborazo, the highest mountain of Ecuador at 20,500 feet and Mt. Cotopaxi at 19,165 feet.

Serge, the Rower

In 1999, Serge kayaked 260 miles of the super-treacherous white water of the Nahanni River in the Northwest Territories of Canada. In the winter of 2011, Serge and Ole Elmer launched a twenty-two-foot by five-foot canoe off the coast of the Canary Islands. Sixty-three days and 3,500 miles later, they had rowed their way across the open Atlantic Ocean (with no back-up support) and docked in Barbados.

Serge, the Boxer

Serge is a six-time Swiss National Boxing Champion (1973, 1975, 1976, 1977, 1980, and 1982). He earned a spot on the 1976 Swiss Olympic Team. However, because of financial misconduct by a Swiss boxing official, the team was precluded from participating. He calls this the greatest disappointment of his life.

Serge, the Bicyclist

In 1978, over the course of nine months, Serge rode an 11,200-mile sightseeing and endurance trip which started in Montreal. He experienced the wonder and beauty of North America as he zigzagged toward the west coast of the United States. Having arrived at the coast, he then turned east and rode a zigzag route to Florida.

Serge, the Machete Wielder

In 1996, during the American Challenge, over the course of twelve days, Serge and a German man, Uwe Diemer, macheteed their way across one hundred miles of the incredibly treacherous and dense jungle of the Darien Gap, one of the most rugged and dangerous places on earth. There is no road through the Gap, only swamps, rainforest, and mountains. It is infested with irate guerrillas, crazed drug lords and drug traffickers, greedy kidnappers, paranoid government agents, and a host of dangerous animals.

Serge, the Humanitarian

In addition to his physical endurance feats, Serge has always had a tremendous heart for helping others. With the help of Nicole, Serge has raised awareness about the plight of children around the world, financially supporting the education of a group of street children in Bolivia and continually supporting Dr. Ron Zamber's nonprofit foundation, International Vision Quest, which restores vision and treats eye disease for thousands of individuals in developing nations. During the World Tour, Serge and Nicole joined Dr. Zamber and his team on an eye-care mission to Costa Rica.

Serge is an associate of The Roetheli Lil' Red Foundation, and in conjunction with Food for the Poor, this foundation has built nearly 300 homes, four schools, four water-supply systems, four community/worship centers, and four stores in Guyana, South America–the second poorest country in the western hemisphere. He also spent part of his early career serving as a counselor for young individuals with addictions.

To join in the discussion of his feats, please visit the Roetheli Lil' Red Foundation (www.lilredfoundation.com) and comment on the blog. We'd love to hear your impressions of Serge and who you think is the greatest endurance athlete of all time. He certainly has our vote, but then again, he also has our heart.

Serge has always said, "Impossible is just a stupid word." We hope his persistent attitude and his amazing accomplishments are as contagious and affective for you as they have been for us.

The 25,000 Mile Love Story Creative Team
> Rob Pafundi
> Christy Dreiling
> John Davies
> Brian Kallies
> Priscilla Pesci
> David Dunham

The Roetheli Lil' Red Foundation Representatives
> Joe and Judy Roetheli
> Agnes Roetheli Gaertner
> Melissa Place

To learn more about Serge and his accomplishments, please visit our websites:
> www.the25000milelovestory.com
> www.lilredfoundation.org

We would also encourage you to read the other great stories about Serge and Nicole in Nicole's account of the World Tour, *Nicole's Diary: Running the World . . . Losing Our Marbles,* and the beautiful full-color coffee-table book by Serge and Nicole, *Keep on Running: The American Challenge.*

Appendix

The World Tour By the Numbers

Days on the Road: 1,910

Months on the Road:. 63

Total Miles Run:. 25,422

Number of Continents:. 6

Number of Countries:. 35

Nights Spent in a Tent: . . . . >1,200

Smiles Brought to Kids' Faces: . . . . Tens of thousands

Eyes Cared for in Costa Rica:. 592

Tons of Coca Cola Consumed: 6

Pairs of Shoes Used: 64

Tubes of Lipstick Nicole Used: 101

Times each of Serge's Feet Pounded the Road: . . . . ~33,600,000

Times Clara and Steve visited Serge on the Tour 8

Dollars Raised for Kids: $420,000